Honored Feathers of Wisdom

Jiva,
I hope you find this interesting.
Regards,
Tim

Honored Feathers of Wisdom

✦

Attributes For Personal And Organizational Growth

Robert L. Boggs, PH.D.

iUniverse, Inc.
New York Lincoln Shanghai

Honored Feathers of Wisdom
Attributes For Personal And Organizational Growth

iUniverse, Inc.

For information address:
iUniverse, Inc.
2021 Pine Lake Road, Suite 100
Lincoln, NE 68512
www.iuniverse.com

ISBN: 0-595-29991-1 (pbk)
ISBN: 0-595-66104-1 (cloth)

Printed in the United States of America

This book is dedicated to my lovely and talented wife Cindy. I was forever blessed the day I met her. I also dedicate this book to my daughter Fleming and my son Sage. These three are the loves of my life.

Contents

FOREWORD

The wisdom of Native Americans is a great blessing from the past and an unparalleled opportunity for the present. Much of what we know about the attributes of Native American wisdom comes to us through myths and folklore. It was through oratory, rather than the written word, that they passed along the attributes of wisdom from generation to generation.

Like other indigenous cultures, the wisdom of Native Americans was not a matter of philosophical debate or conjecture. Their wisdom was a deeply imbedded part of their everyday life. Luckily, there are those who have been willing to share their knowledge so that we may learn more about cultures that understood the importance of community leadership, the uniqueness of each individual, and the symbiotic relationship between humans and nature.

A timeless connection exists between Native American wisdom, personal development, and the direction organizations must take in order to provide healthy, happy, and productive work environments. Understanding and practicing the attributes of wisdom will create dynamic organizations to propel us through the 21st century.

In my search for Native American attributes of wisdom, I tried to locate Nokoma Volkman, the artist who designed the parchment "Pathway to Wisdom." I called Native American artist associations and searched the Internet. Many people had heard of Volkman and were familiar with his work but no one knew how to reach him.

Then serendipity came into play. In a conversation with a Native American woman who worked as a librarian at my son's elementary school, I mentioned Volkman's parchment. I told her how impressed I was by his visual interpretation of wisdom and how much I would like to talk with him. She had some of his work at home and knew how to reach him. After months of fruitless searching, I found the information I needed just three miles from the front door of my home. My research was about to begin in earnest.

Volkman and I agreed to meet at a pow-wow in Xenia, Ohio. I discovered that he was an artist, writer, lecturer, singer and traditional dancer. His work was strongly influenced by his Anishinabe-Lakota cultural traditions. He grew up in Wisconsin, graduated from North Central College, and served overseas in the

Peace Corps. Volkman became a proud member of the LaDeux family, direct descendents of Chief Red Cloud of the Oglala Lakota Sioux.

His interpretation of wisdom was based upon many lessons he had learned from his Native American heritage and wide range of life long experiences. We concurred on many of the steps that led a person towards personal development and wisdom. He wished me luck on my journey along the *Good Red Road*. It was now time to learn more about earning the *Honored Feathers of Wisdom*.

I learned more about the Native American perspective of wisdom from Rainbow Eagle, author of *The Universal Peace Shield of Truths: Ancient American Indian Peace Shield Teachings*. He describes the Seven Gifts of the Sacred People symbolized by eagle feathers. The Seven Gifts are:

> Wisdom: to cherish knowledge is to know wisdom.
>
> Love: to know love is to know peace.
>
> Respect: to honor all of the Creation is to have respect.
>
> Courage/Bravery: Bravery is to face the foe with integrity.
>
> Honesty: Honesty in facing a situation is to be brave.
>
> Humility: Humility is to know your self as a sacred part of the Creation.
>
> Truth: Truth is to know all of these things.

There are several common attributes that appear when you seek the true nature of Native American wisdom. The attributes of wisdom are cross-cultural and traverse time and space.

> "Across cultures and epochs, literature calls for justice, honesty, tolerance, compassion, generosity, self-discipline, and courage. The Golden Mean has been a reference point for centuries to help us find balance in our lives between wants and needs…wisdom capital is a community's common ground."
>
> —Claire L. Gaudiani

The Bible also addresses attributes of wisdom. According to Galatians 5: 22–23, the fruits of the spirit are love, joy, peace, patience, kindness, generosity, faithfulness, gentleness, and self control.

Native Americans couldn't understand why European settlers tried to convert them to their religious beliefs. Native Americans already understood and practiced what was being taught in Galatians. Unfortunately, it has taken hundreds of years to fully appreciate and understand the valuable lessons of a thoughtful and spiritually advanced culture.

It is important that we understand and practice these attributes of wisdom: appreciation, cheerfulness, compassion, courage, determination, dialogue, experience, honesty, humility, justice, kindness, knowledge, leadership, loyalty, patience, respect, sacrifice, sharing, and vision.

These attributes enable rather than hinder people and their organizations. Wisdom tradition recognizes the uniqueness of others? Discovering the uniqueness of others is achieved by recognizing shared attributes of wisdom.

This book addresses the attributes of wisdom as practiced in the Native American cultures of the past. It is not a study of today's Native American cultures but a study of the cultures that existed in their purest form when Native American society flourished in the woodlands, mountains, and plains of North America. This is not a political indictment against past wrongs or future political imperatives; rather, it is an attempt to understand the value of unique cultures that effectively practiced the attributes of wisdom.

ACKNOWLEDGEMENTS

This book was written with the help of several talented people. They are all close friends whom I deeply admire. I thank Dr. Samuel C. Heady for his continued support and friendship. Sam's sense of humor, understanding of human nature and all things academic has been a great help. I thank Dr. Mace Ishida for his insights and thoughtful comments. Mace contributed unselfishly of his time while providing many ideas incorporated in this work. A special thank you goes to my dear friend Dr. Mark Pitstick. We became lifelong friends the first day we met. Mark's attention to detail and willingness to share his time and talent greatly improved this book. I thank Dr. Mary Jo Wetterich for her boundless energy and enthusiasm. She is an inspiring person who deeply understands and practices wisdom. I'm very grateful to Robert C. Albright for his helpful comments and support. Bob is well versed in the art of leadership and shares my passion for teaching. I'd also like to thank Steve Momper for his helpful comments and willingness to share his time and expertise. Finally, I gladly acknowledge a lady of exceptional talent, my wife Cindy. She provided invaluable advice on content and structure. Her limitless talent, love, and support helped make this book possible.

INTRODUCTION

It was a cool August morning on Lake Huron as I looked out over the waves that moved between the shores of the Michigan mainland and my destination, Macinac Island. I was on the upper deck of the early morning ferry that was taking me on a short trip in order to explore the interesting sites of this remote historic area. The island still had a fort that traced its history back to the struggles between the early European settlers, the British Empire, and the Native American inhabitants.

I chose this island for a brief respite, not knowing that my trip would lead to an idea that would culminate in the writing of this book. While writing about the values of community service as one form of leadership I discovered something important. I found a culture that truly understood and valued community service, that venerated those who practiced community service, and selected leaders based on their willingness to help others. The culture I'm referring to is Native American.

I have been fascinated with leadership issues as long as I can remember. My shelves are lined with the seminal works of dozens of authors. Much of what these authors have written is profound. Yet something was missing from all their magical formulas for leadership success.

Many of these authors believe if you do certain things, you will be a great leader and people will treat you with great adulation. You will reap enormous fortune, and your very presence will inspire all of those around you. Yet the formulas for leadership success always left me a bit cold. I knew in my heart that great leaders didn't carry around some all-powerful, awe-inspiring leadership checklist that would ensure them and their followers a lifetime of success and happiness. It isn't quite that easy.

While reflecting on all this, I happened upon a small Native American shop. As an adult I have felt strongly drawn to Native American culture: Maybe because the land I live upon was once traversed by the Shawnee and the Iroquois; maybe because the distant history of my own family traces its ancestry back to the Cherokee. Or maybe, it was an inkling that we can learn much from past cultures that still impact our personal and organizational development.

While browsing, I discovered a parchment by a Native American Sioux named Nokoma Volkman. Volkman had created a piece of artwork called "Pathway to

Wisdom". On the parchment "Wisdom" was drawn in a small circle with the quill of feathers pointing towards the circle. Each of the feathers had a word drawn on it that was one of the attributes needed to achieve a balanced life in the Sacred Circle. That moment, I realized the real issue for self-development was not in becoming a better leader. The real issue was in becoming a wiser person.

The attributes that lead to wisdom are many. We are all better at some attributes than others; we may excel at some and never truly excel at others. It is in acquiring these attributes of wisdom that we become true leaders. We become leaders who don't require positional power in order to influence others.

This book is about the attributes of wisdom that lead to personal and organizational growth. Leaders throughout history exhibited these characteristics. Native American leaders exhibited these qualities over the centuries. These attributes are timeless, and they are needed more now than ever.

If you understand the attributes of wisdom and are willing to practice them, you will be a leader. You will be the type of leader that others will follow willingly. You will be the type of leader that is needed to succeed in the 21st Century.

PATHWAY TO WISDOM

This book will take you on a journey that was traversed by the great Native American chiefs of old. If Tecumseh, Chief Joseph, or Sitting Bull were with us today, they would explain that we are all in a constant state of transformation. They would also express that our transformation is likened to following a path along a sacred circle that has no beginning or end.

What you can expect to learn is that wisdom is not acquired through philosophical debate or conjecture. True wisdom is acquired through personal acts that coincide with the 19 attributes of wisdom in this book. Be aware that acts associated with these attributes must be reinforced through ceremony and celebration. Further, when you or others perform an act that leads to greater personal wisdom, that achievement should be recognized and rewarded.

You will see how Native Americans used feathers as a symbol of achievement. The giving of feathers was how they recognized those who successfully underwent personal transformations. It is the feather that best symbolizes the attainment of each of the attributes of wisdom.

You will understand that you have been empowered to take your own unique journey along the sacred circle. You are the shaman (visionary) who hastens your own transformation. It is up to you to assess whether changes are needed for attaining greater wisdom.

At the end of each section you will find suggestions on how to earn an Honored Feather of Wisdom for each attribute. These suggestions are in no way all inclusive. You may already be practicing these and other important attributes of wisdom in your life. Don't hesitate to add other attributes of wisdom to the list. This is your journey; you are a trailblazer on a path of personal transformation.

The chiefs of old successfully followed their own path. Through personal growth and development they became the manifestation of wisdom for their tribe. You must do the same if you are to earn the Honored Feathers of Wisdom.

NATIVE AMERICAN WISDOM

o o o o o o o o o o o o o o o o o o o o o o o o o o o o o o o o o

"The human maturity process is not linear, because life is a circle or wheel, reminding us that wherever we go and whatever we experience, the self is still present when we arrive, bringing us home to ourselves and all that we have become during our learning process."

—Jamie Sams,
Dancing the Dream

Wisdom is acquired when we balance what we have learned intellectually with what we know emotionally. This marriage of intellect and emotion allows us to acquire true wisdom and provides the balance needed to evolve as human beings. In doing so, we have the opportunity to elevate the rest of society even though many do not yet grasp the significance of intellectual and emotional balance.

The uniquely balanced Native American cultures offered distinctive opportunities for personal and organizational growth. Many organizations today understand the significance of balance. Community involvement, respect for the environment, quality management, exceptional customer service, and good employee relations all contribute to the aggregate of organizational success. Today, many communities are more prosperous than others because their citizens act like members of a tribe. They volunteer more, sing together and play together, which allows the community to bond, trust and prosper.

We are all part of diverse and varied communities. In my own small village, people work together to provide for their needs and for others. The school principal is a Cub Scout Master, the grocer is a church elder, the parent who stays home with young children also serves on committees and councils. In this interactive environment, those who live there meet the needs of the community.

Wall and Arden (1990) conducted an interview with eighty-four year old Vernon Cooper during their visit to the Lumbee in 1989. The Lumbee are the largest Indian tribe east of the Mississippi and one of the least known. According to the authors, historians theorize that the Lumbee's ancestors absorbed the missing white settlers of the famous "Lost Colony" founded by Sir Walter Raleigh on the Virginia coast in the late 16th century.

Lumbee elder Vernon Cooper shared his thoughts with the authors on the concept of wisdom:

> "I just wasn't cut out for the age we're living in. Everybody's hurrying but nobody's going anywhere. People aren't living, they're only existing. They're growing away from spiritual realities. These days people seek knowledge, not wisdom. Knowledge is of the past; wisdom is of the future. We're in an age now when people are slumbering. They think they're awake, yet they're really sleeping. But this is a dangerous age, the most dangerous in human history. People need to wake up. They can't hear God's voice if they're asleep."

Native American wisdom is *spiritual wisdom*. It isn't learned in a book, it is lived day by day. It is a holistic combination of intellectual and emotional growth. Wisdom doesn't come from reading about acts of kindness, it comes from being kind. Wisdom doesn't come from understanding the concept of honesty, it comes from being honest. To earn the Honored Feathers of Wisdom you don't just read or understand the attributes of wisdom, you live them.

Native American culture is prodigiously influenced by symbolism. The Honored Feathers of Wisdom can be visualized as part of a circle known as a *Medicine Wheel*.

> "You have noticed that everything an Indian does is in a circle, and that is because the power of the world always works in circles, and everything tries to be round…the sky is round, and I have heard the earth is round like a ball, and so are all the stars. The wind, in its greatest power, whirls. Birds make their nest in circles, for theirs is the same religion as ours…even the seasons form a great circle in their changing, and always come back again to where they were. The life of a man is a circle from childhood to childhood, and so it is in everything where power moves."
>
> —Black Elk

The circle symbolizes a continuous path that has no beginning and no ending. If we visualize our lives as part of a *sacred circle*, we realize that our past, present, and future are all connected. A Medicine Wheel is a sacred circle that can be used to help visualize and assist with personal change and growth. It symbolizes the never-ending path we follow in order to grow and change throughout the course of our lives. It is through embracing change that personal growth is attained.

The creation and use of Medicine Wheels date back to ancient times. Native American Medicine Wheels were used in the Great Plains and Rocky Mountains of the United States and Canada. The great stone circles of the Celts and the mandalas of India are cross-cultural versions of the Medicine Wheel. The Medicine Wheel is often associated with prayer, meditation, contemplation and the search for understanding of self and our connectedness with all creation.

To understand the Medicine Wheel we can look at the principles of Cangleska Wakan as explained by Emmett C. Murphy and Michael Snell (1994). In the Sioux culture, the Sacred Hoop encompasses all things that make up the universe. The hoop is a state of being, an understanding of the universe that connects all things in a mutual destiny.

To the Sioux, the circle symbolizes the belief that all things participate in one ordered whole, sharing the same physical and spiritual space. It embraces the idea of inclusion and the potential for everything within the circle to grow and change. Each point in the circle represents the interrelationships that comprise the universe. Like a compass, the four points of the circle signify the directions of the earth. Each point also represents a state of mind or understanding.

The Medicine Wheel symbolizes our journey through life. We begin our life at some point on the Medicine Wheel. We are born with certain gifts and abilities that, over time, will be developed as we gain experience and knowledge. Throughout our life we travel around the Medicine Wheel striving for wisdom, seeking illumination, regaining our innocence and learning through introspection. It is during this life-long journey that we change and grow.

The Sioux and other Native American tribes were fluid cultures that understood the nature of change. They understood interconnectedness because that is how they lived their lives. They were a part of the constantly changing fabric of the world.

The essence of the Medicine Wheel is change and growth. Everything in nature continually changes and as part of nature, humans also must change. We are afraid of change even though change leads to personal growth. Those who live in a natural way accept and embrace the changes they experience. They see change as a way of life. Unfortunately, society today sees change as a threat rather than an opportunity for growth. But change is natural and can't be held in abeyance for any significant length of time. We can no more delay our own transitions than we can the changing of the seasons. Change is inevitable, and in Native American cultures, change was cause for celebration and ceremony.

Ceremony is commonly defined as some type of formal act performed by a prescribed ritual. Ceremony is a way to give back to creation a portion of what we have received or hope to receive. We see ceremony in many aspects of our lives. Two places where we commonly see the use of ceremony is in the practice of religious and military traditions. Our traditions are peppered with ceremonies of one type or another. Bear, Wind, and Mulligan (1991) stress the importance of ceremonies. In their words:

> "Through ceremony, we learn how to give back. When we sing, we give energy through our voice; when we drum, we allow the earth's heartbeat to join with our own; when we dance, we bring the energy of the earth and sky together in our bodies and give it out; when we pray, we give energy through our hearts; when we look upon our relations, we give blessings through our eyes. When we put all these activities together, we have ceremony, one of the most powerful forms of gift-giving we humans possess."

The ancients knew the importance of ceremony. Throughout the year they celebrated with seasonal ceremonies, deer dances, strawberry festivals, corn festivals, bear dances, full moon ceremonies and thanksgiving celebrations. These were not arbitrary events but, rather, well-planned and meaningful rituals for those who participated.

Today, we still have traditions and celebrations that are remotely linked to those of our ancestors. We observe our national and religious holidays despite the lack of sacredness.

Ceremonies are not restricted to just the church or military. Ceremony can be cross culturally assimilated. One example of this was evidenced at a Pow-Wow where a Native American Color Guard performed. These veterans presented Old Glory in a way that made me rethink the sacredness of the American Flag and all it stands for. You could feel the energy and passion in the ceremony as the veterans danced around the flagpole. The music, dancing, and dedication turned what could have been just another well-intentioned event into a sacred ceremony.

Ceremony is a way of giving back, of showing our appreciation, a very personal type of gift giving. There is a need to celebrate what we hold to be sacred. Our ancestors understood this and we also need to understand. Sacred ceremonies need to be a part of our communities. The ancients celebrated the changing seasons, the harvesting of crops, and the accomplishments of their people. Many organizations are now beginning to understand the wisdom of celebrations. We celebrate a lucrative sale, a new product, or a new innovation through celebration. By gathering our work community together to share in our accomplishments, we plant the seed of celebration. By recognizing specific acts of individuals and groups, we make celebration a part of our culture. Through the proliferation of ceremony and celebration we become self-aware of our accomplishments and contributions of others.

Ceremony is how we celebrate the achievement of wisdom. This is particularly true when we earn the Honored Feathers of Wisdom. Each and every feather we earn brings us closer to wisdom. Acquiring greater wisdom is worth celebrating.

Ceremony, the celebration that accompanies it, and the symbols we use to represent accomplishments are intricately connected. The feather serves as a symbol of accomplishment. Symbolism allows us to represent ideas or concepts through objects, events, or relationships. Native Americans were symbolists who successfully interpreted or represented conditions or truths by the use of symbols.

> "Let a man decide upon his favorite animal and make a study of it…let him learn to understand its sounds and motions. The animals want to communicate with man, but Wakan-Tanka does not intend they shall do so directly-man must do the greater part in securing an understanding."
>
> —Brave Buffalo

"Realizing that visible bodies are only symbols of invisible forces, the ancients worshipped the Divine Power through the lower kingdoms of Nature...The sages of old studied living things to a point of realization that God is most perfectly understood through a knowledge of His supreme handiwork-animate and inanimate Nature. Every existing creature manifests some aspect of the intelligence or power of the Eternal One."

—Manly P. Hall,
The Secret Teachings of All Ages

Out of necessity, an interaction takes place between the people of nomadic hunting cultures and animals that share their habitat. The observation of animal traits were a prime medium through which cultures expressed their core values. Joseph Epes Brown (1997) believes that the values of generosity, creativity, and strength seem not to be projected onto the bison but to emanate from it. He goes on to say, "The correspondences between the animal traits and the human values were as if one were the reflection of the other; they flowed into each other in a manner that expresses a total, integrated environment. These strong associations gave the Oglala excellent models for practical skills and desired qualities of human personality."

Symbology helped shape Native American cultural values. A dominant part of this culture is relationship. Relationships extended from the individual to the immediate family, the extended family, the band, the clan, and on to the tribe. Native American culture differed from Western culture in that their relationships didn't stop at the human realm as ours do today. Their relationships extended out to include the whole environment. They had a relationship with the environment, the plants, animals, wind, stars, and literally the entire universe.

In 1904, Chief Letakos-Lesa of the Pawnee Tribe explained, "In the beginning of all things, wisdom and knowledge were with the animals; for Tuawa, the *One Above*, did not speak directly to man. He sent animals to tell man that he showed himself through the beasts, and that from them, and from the stars and the sun and the moon, man should learn...for all things speak of Tuawa."

Native Americans lived on the land and were inseparable from all of nature. A symbiotic relationship existed and was expressed in the way people dressed (the wearing of feathers and fetishes), decorated their lodges, medicine shields and other belongings. The paints that adorned their bodies and possessions were an expression of their unique relationship to nature. A fetish is an object believed to have magical powers or an object that receives attention or reverence.

According to Native American belief, each animal has its own unique characteristics. We can learn a great deal about ourselves through animals. We can take the lessons from the animals and apply them to our everyday lives. *Heiku Owusu* in her book *Symbols of Native America*, helps us understand the symbology of animals. For example, if we lack a spirit of generosity and sharing, we can develop characteristics symbolized by the turkey. The turkey teaches us about sharing because it gives up its life so that others may live. We come together to give thanks and, in so doing, it is the turkey that gives us sustenance.

In Heiku Owusu's opinion, if we lack self-confidence, we can take on the characteristic of the skunk. The skunk appears to be self-assured and confident of its own power. It is through the sense of smell rather than physical prowess that we respect the skunk. If we become more like the roe deer and give unconditional love; more like the ant and support our community; more like the hummingbird by spreading joy and happiness wherever we go; we are bound to become wiser human beings. Native American symbolism segues into the Honored Feathers of Wisdom.

For Native Americans, it was the shaman who understood the connection between daily life and the natural and spiritual worlds.

> "In the past shamans, priests, and priestesses were the keepers of the sacred knowledge of life. These individuals were tied to the rhythms and forces of nature. They were capable of walking the threads that link the invisible and visible worlds. They helped people remember that all trees are divine and that all animals speak to those who listen."
>
> —Ted Andrews, *Animal-Speak*

In Native American tradition, the shaman helped connect our conscious human life with the natural world and the world of spirit. The shaman was someone who could see into the sacred world and share their vision with the people. The shaman used a ritual process that included storytelling, music, dance and art for expression. In a world where humanity was considered a part of nature; where you did not distinguish between natural and supernatural; where dreams were as real as waking hours; the role of the shaman was critical to the well being of the culture.

In Celtic tradition, the term "shaman" can be translated as meaning "to burn up, to set on fire." This referred to the ability of the shaman to work with the energy of heat. Other meanings of the word shaman are "one who is excited, moved, raised up." It has also been traced to the Indo-European root word meaning "to know" or sometimes "to heat oneself." Most importantly, shamans continually shaped and honed their spiritual selves to develop better and more lasting ways of encountering and interacting with dimensions of the sacred.

Judeo-Christian theology teaches us that we are corrupt beings who are separated from spiritual realms and have fallen from grace. Those raised in the Judeo-Christian tradition are deeply influenced by these beliefs. The shamanic viewpoint was based on a fundamental understanding that people were an integral part of the observable natural and spiritual world.

When we are on a path of shaping and honing our personal growth we are in effect, shamans. When we follow the pathway toward wisdom, we are on the path of the shaman.

Organizations today don't have a "Chief of Shamanism." Instead, they have "Chief Executive Officers, "Chief Financial Officers," "Chief of Operations," or in the more progressive companies, "Chief Knowledge Officer." The very issues addressed by the shaman of old (connecting our conscious human life with the natural world and the world of spirit) are still critical for personal and organizational development today. A "Chief of Shamanism" would have to be part psychologist, psychiatrist, chaplain, psychic, dancer, motivational speaker, and mystic. With that in mind, there shouldn't be any problem advertising for or selecting a qualified shaman after a thorough review by Human Resources.

To varying degrees, we are all on paths of personal growth. We want to be excited and moved by something. Learning new skills is valuable for personal and organizational development. Most of all, we desire a sense of well-being.

Today, more than ever, we need shamans in our organizations. We seek people who are willing to help others by listening and assisting them to reach their full potential. We want people who are aware of their physical and non-physical surroundings. We crave people that understand the importance and purpose of knowledge and the need to share that wisdom with others.

The role of the shaman today is just as important as it was when humanity still recognized itself as part of nature. It may seem archaic to think of shamans in modern organizations but modern scientific discoveries teach that the physical (visible), spiritual (invisible) are connected even though they don't necessarily show up on an organizational chart.

The most obvious physical manifestation of the attributes of wisdom could be seen in those individuals selected to lead their tribes. The chiefs of old proudly wore the Honored Feathers of Wisdom because of their accomplishments.

As early as 1805, the journals of Meriwether Lewis and William Clark provide some insight into the role of the Native American chief.

"Each individual is his own master, and the only control to which his conduct is subjected is the advice of a chief, supported by his influence over the rest of the tribe." The chief's power was far from being absolute. In fact, the commands of the chief had no effect on those who were inclined to disobey them.

It was only through earning the respect of his peers that a man could become a chief. One way to be considered for the position of chief was to prove to be a great warrior by winning eagle feathers for acts of bravery. Yet chiefs were also known for their idealism and cooperation.

According to *Time Life Books* (1975), *The Great Chiefs*, in selecting a chief, the Kiowa Council identified the many qualities they looked for in a principal chief. To begin with:

> "He must have a record of outstanding accomplishment in war; although in his new role he would not himself be a tactical leader, he would be expected to set an example of courage if circumstance brought war to his people. He must possess a compelling personality that would draw others to him and inspire their loyalty and respect. Indeed, respect was his sole source of power, and to be truly effective he must be a man of great wealth—the owner of many horses obtained by leading raids. Moreover, he must have demonstrated his generosity by giving feasts and providing food, horses and buffalo hides to those who were less fortunate than he was.
>
> Finally, he must be energetic, equable of temper, receptive to the opinions of others, deliberate in reaching judgments and gifted with an eloquent tongue. These traits would be indispensable in carrying out his primary duties: suggesting the division of hunting assignments when the tribe separated, acting as spokesman in meetings with other tribes, mediating factional and personal disputes within the tribe, and at all times encouraging the unity of his people."

Selecting a chief needed to be a unanimous or nearly unanimous decision. This was the basis of tribal decision-making. Although some chiefs inherited their position from their fathers, chieftainship among the Plains tribes usually was nonhereditary. In all tribes, it was essentially the man who made the office. Individuals of deep conviction, forceful character and proven ability stood out and were recognized as great chiefs.

According to Clark and Friswod (1976), Chief He Dog of the Oglala Sioux looked for the following four characteristics in order to be made a chief.

• He must be brave and out-spoken.

• He must be ambitious.

- He must be honest at all times.

- He must be kind to all creatures.

The newly elected chief received a beaded buckskin outfit, an eagle feather to wear in his hair and a pipe and tobacco bags. The wise old men of the tribe then lectured the new chief on his responsibilities. If the chief did not obey the four rules, he was ordered out of the tribe for five years. After five years he was given another opportunity to become a chief. The five-year banishment was a punishment and an opportunity to acquire the experience needed to become a chief. Anyone who disobeyed the four rules again was ordered out of the tribe for good.

There were no set time limits on how long someone could be chief as long as he behaved himself properly. According to Rev. Eagle Hawk, a man was made chief and lectured on the following points:

- he should remember there are a lot of wasps and flies that sting, and beware lest they sting and confuse him

- he should remember that there are a lot of dogs that will bark and defile his dwelling place but he shouldn't pay any attention to them

- if one of his close kin is killed in battle, he must not stop to look lest he feel the need to retaliate and it is considered disgraceful for him to lose his temper

- he must not be stingy with his food and he must feed everyone who visits him

- he must offer tobacco to whomever visits him

Crazy Horse was one of several exemplary chiefs who lived by the rules that applied to Sioux chieftains. Crazy Horse was loved and valued by his people as much for his charity as for his courage. The great historian George E. Hyde was mystified by the legend of Crazy Horse and saw him as both a lover of peace and genius at warfare.

> "Crazy Horse was given the great honor of being a Shirt-wearer. This was a position of great responsibility. As a Shirt-wearer he was responsible for providing for the weak and the helpless ones in his tribe. According to those that knew him, he was one of the great chiefs that never forgot his responsibility to his people. Even though, in the end, it cost him his life."

Native American chiefs were known for exhibiting many attributes of wisdom. They were an integral part of their communities and were selected to guide their people because they exhibited attributes needed for survival. Attributes these indigenous people valued are missing from many organizations today.

We've all heard "there are too many chiefs and not enough Indians around here." The truth is, there are very few chiefs anywhere and modern organizations especially need more chiefs. We need people in our organizations that understand and practice the attributes valued by Native American societies. Attributes needed for tribal chiefs are identical to those needed for today's organizational leaders.

Would you follow a person who is brave, out-spoken, ambitious, honest, and kind? Would you admire a person who is energetic, equable of temper, receptive to the opinions of others, deliberate in reaching judgments and gifted of eloquent tongue? These are just some of the attributes expected of a chief and needed by leaders. Native American cultures respected these attributes and showed their respect by presenting an Honored Feather of Wisdom when it was earned. Let us more closely examine this concept of Honored Feathers of Wisdom.

Reflective thoughts

HONORED FEATHERS OF WISDOM

o o o o o o o o o o o o o o o o o o o o o o o o o o o o o o o

"To Native Americans, the feather is universally symbolic. It is found in all aspects of life-from ceremonial use reflecting tribal philosophies and religions to functional and ornamental uses. It is attached to all the activities of living: making rain, planting and harvesting crops, success in fishing, protecting homes, curing illness. Considered to be the "breath of life," the feather possesses the power and spirit of the bird of which it once was a living part."

—Gail Tuchman

To honor someone is to show high regard or appreciation for an act or accomplishment that distinguishes the individual. Honoring someone entails the conferring of an adornment that symbolizes an accomplishment. The military has honored acts of bravery and allegiance for centuries. Medals and ribbons are worn on the uniforms of military members as evidence of service to their nation and the principles they practice and hold in high esteem.

Native American cultures also honored the accomplishment of others. The way they honored others was closely tied to their deep respect for and understanding of nature. Rather than using medals or ribbons, they bestowed feathers to show high regard or appreciation. Feathers symbolized the attributes that were honored by native peoples.

They believed all living things had value. They believed by studying all living things and by studying our four legged and feathered relatives they learned lessons for personal growth. This is why native people wore or carried animal or bird fetishes. They were reminders of what they accomplished or hoped to accomplish in their lives.

Symbolism invests objects with meaning. Objects can symbolize the invisible, the intangible, or the spiritual. They can indicate qualities, powers, or the attributes we value.

Objects used as symbols vary from culture to culture. Feathers were commonly used as symbols in Native American culture. Tuchman (1994) explains the significance of feathers and what they symbolized to Native Americans:

> "Each individual uses different feathers (wing feathers, tail feathers) from different birds (each with its own symbolism and energy) in different ways for different purposes (blessing, awakening, cleansing, healing)-depending on his or her own beliefs, knowledge, perceptions, and experiences."

The types and parts of feathers used by tribes were as varied as the tribes themselves. Lakota Sioux ceremonially awarded a feather to members of the tribe when they earned it. There were feathers for every occasion. Feathers were used for making rain, for success in hunting and fishing, for protection of homes and for curing the sick. Feathers were used in lullabies, love songs, corn grinding, and social dancing. Feathers were earned for acts of bravery, wisdom, fortitude, and generosity.

Among the Cherokee, feathers were awarded for certain achievements. Tribal members wore feathers based on specific actions they performed such as overcoming a serious personal limitation or fear.

For some tribes, the quill of a feather symbolized the concept of balance. This balance was a goal in life, a relationship to the forces of the universe which one hopes to enhance or prolong daily life. It was believed when a person disrupted the balance of harmony, they created disorder and risked mental anguish, physical torment and even death. To restore the balance, ceremonies were conducted that involved the use of feathers.

For other tribes, the quill symbolized the path of the heart while the feathering part that branches out from the quill, represented decisions made in life's journey. Even the down feathers of birds had a special meaning to Native Americans. Down feathers were seen as a bridge between Mother Earth and the spirit world. They were used to mark sacred sites and to ask for blessings.

A shaman purified every feather. In this way the recipient of the feather would not catch the badness of the feather. A blessed feather could be passed on to someone else and was about the highest gift you could receive. A blessed feather received as a gift exceeded the value of money.

Feathers were used to represent the attributes of wisdom. Conrad House in his book, *All Roads are Good* said:

> "How you live life is both an art and religion, as is how you treat and respect the environment-including animals, plants, and fellow humans-all life forms, even our Mother Earth. We see no need to create concepts to separate or fragment our daily lives. You need not have to go to church and pray when your home and environment are your church, your place of prayers. Try to live a clean, beautiful, good, and balanced life. Be generous and caring. That's what our elders tell us."

The Honored Feathers of Wisdom symbolize the many positive attributes of Native American culture. These attributes have great value and provide each of us with an opportunity for personal growth and development. To do this, we must begin by understanding what the attributes of wisdom are.

The attributes that have a common link in Native American cultures are: *appreciation*; *cheerfulness*; *compassion*; *courage*; *determination*; *dialogue*; *experience*; *honesty*; *humility*; *justice*; *kindness*; *knowledge*; *leadership*; *loyalty*; *patience*; *respect*; *sacrifice*; *sharing*; and *vision*.

Just as Native American cultures bestowed feathers to honor the accomplishments of others, we can also honor ourselves for practicing these attributes of wisdom. Even today, feathers can symbolize the attributes that are honored within our society. Knowing what the attributes are is not the same as understanding or practicing them. It is through the application of these attributes that we earn the

Honored Feathers of Wisdom. In this book, you will learn about each of the attributes of wisdom. You will gain insights into how Native American leaders from the past exhibited the attributes of wisdom. You will also gain an understanding of how you can earn the Honored Feathers of Wisdom.

Reflective thoughts

THE FUNCTIONS OF THE CHIEF

There are 19 attributes of wisdom from the Native American past. The chiefs of old, when practicing these attributes, were functioning as a *bestower*, *companion* and *guide*. The following is a brief explanation of each of the three functions and their associated attributes of wisdom.

Bestower

The first function of a chief is that of a bestower. The bestower is a benefactor, someone who gives freely to others and gives without asking for something in return. The bestower puts several attributes of wisdom to good use. In a philanthropic culture where it was truly better to give than to receive, chiefs were expected to practice the attributes *compassion, kindness, patience, respect, sacrifice* and *sharing*.

Compassion for others is one of the greatest characteristics a person can have. Too often, we see compassion as a weakness rather than as strength. In the Native American culture of the past, a chief who lacked compassion didn't stay a chief for very long. Great leaders can make mercy and compassion a key element in their formula for success. To do this, leaders must be cognizant of who their people are and discern what they are going through.

Kindness has to do with the ability to use both your mind and heart when dealing with others. Without kindness, leaders eventually lose the respect of their followers. The myths and stories we want to create about our self and our organization should be ones of altruism that reflects a spirit of kindness. Native American chiefs were public servants who were expected to show big-heartedness to others.

Patience is a virtue that is misunderstood and sometimes punished in a culture that places an ever-increasing value on speed. Native American children were taught to listen and reflect upon everything around them. Chiefs were perceived as stoic because they hesitated to speak until they had effectively listened to what

23

others had to say. When patience is practiced properly, quick fixes are replaced with meaningful and lasting change.

Respect is normally given to what we value. If we give respect unconditionally, we send a strong message that we value the contributions of others. Native American children were taught not to interrupt when someone was speaking. They were also taught to honor visitors, elders, and the physically challenged. To make fun of someone was perceived as a thoughtless act that was corrected immediately with a quiet voice. When we honor others, we honor ourselves. Being respectful brings harmony to organizations.

Sacrifices are made for many different reasons. The really great leaders are the ones who sacrifice the most to attain their dreams. History teaches us that the sacrifices we make today can have a rippling effect that positively impacts the future. The sacrifices of others stand as a testament that validates the need to emulate their example. Good deeds are eventually rewarded.

Finally, the Native American concept of *sharing* was a timeless concept that benefited the entire community. The attribute of sharing was greatly rewarded while greed and selfishness were often punished. It was considered disgraceful to be ungenerous to others. It was said that you could tell who the chief was because he owned the least possessions. Love of possessions was considered a weakness to be overcome. Studies show that leaders who openly share with others gain greater respect from their subordinates. By sharing the things we value most we learn the true meaning of generosity.

Companion

Being a companion is the second function of the chief. A companion is a friend who is easy to relate to. They put you at ease when you are together. They listen intently to what you say while caring about your feelings. Companions make you feel good about yourself. A companion knows you for who you are, overlooking your flaws while celebrating your strengths. Chiefs were companions to their people. As companions, they practiced the attributes of *appreciation*, *cheerfulness*, *dialogue*, *honesty*, *humility*, and *loyalty*.

Appreciation for the good works of others is shown through praise and recognition. Praise and recognition in Native American cultures was given for such noteworthy accomplishments as hard work, providing for the tribe, or an act of bravery. Showing appreciation is one of the smartest and easiest things a leader can do. By being observant and providing timely recognition, a leader can gain the respect and loyalty of their followers.

A *cheerful* leader brings out the cheerfulness in others. They understand the value of humor, laughter, and play. Cheerful leaders are actively engaged in the lives of their people. They bring joy, not sorrow, to the workplace. Native Americans believed humor, laughter, and play were a necessary part of life. A cheerful nature helps us overcome challenges. Humor, laughter, and play are sometimes seen as silly or immature but studies now show they are intricately linked to our physical and emotional health.

Past cultures knew how to *dialogue*. They would gather in a circle and talk until everyone's thoughts had been fully shared. They knew that dialogue was about mutual inquiry and was reflective in nature. Indigenous people understood the sacredness of dialogue in that words had great power. Chiefs such as Tecumseh were considered exceptional communicators because they listened carefully, reflected upon the words of others, then shared their true thoughts through group dialogue.

Honesty is a prerequisite for any type of meaningful relationship. A leader who lacks honesty will also lack followers. Native American cultures required honesty of their leaders. You couldn't attain a position of honor unless you were truthful with your people. Being honest sometimes means telling people things they would rather not hear. The honest leader understands they will be the bearer of unpopular news. Exceptional leaders weigh their words then honestly express themselves in a caring way.

Humility is a quiet acceptance of our own uniqueness and worth. In most native cultures, leaders were known for their unpretentiousness. Humble leaders tend to credit the accomplishment of others while acknowledging their own weaknesses. Silence and solitude are the companions of a modest leader. Taking the time to reflect upon important issues is critical to gaining a self-awareness that leads to a spirit of humility.

Loyalty means being true to yourself and others. The leader who exhibits loyalty will have followers who are willing to confide in them. Being loyal also means being steadfast in our relationships to friends and associates. Faithfulness shouldn't waiver when we are faced with collusion, ridicule, or even violence. To be loyal we must embrace a spirit of tolerance that accepts the shortcomings of others.

Guide

The third function of a chief is that of a guide. A guide is someone who directs others along a desirable path. They have certain, specific or intimate knowledge that is openly shared with their followers. A guide is also a catalyst of change. They are the doers and the visionaries who instill entire organizations with a sense of purpose. Guides do not use threats or force to lead. They are willingly followed because they have earned the trust of others. The attributes of the guide include: *courage*, *determination*, *experience*, *justice*, *knowledge*, *leadership*, and *vision*.

Courage is the strength that allows one to venture, persevere, and withstand danger, fear, or difficulty with unflinching resolution. It is a firmness of spirit that exists during extreme difficulty. Courage is typically attributed to the brave acts of the warrior yet we expect all leaders to be courageous. Acts of bravery are not exclusive to the warrior. Acts of bravery are critical to any organizations success. Leaders must proudly carry their organizational banner while setting an example worth emulating.

Determination is an overwhelming desire to accomplish something of importance. Every culture can name resolute leaders who strove against overwhelming odds in order to turn their dreams into reality. Determined leaders believe in themselves and in the capabilities of their followers. Successful leaders are the ones that guide their followers along the pathway to success even when their critics insist on turning back before the journey ends.

Experience is acquired through direct observation or participation in an event. The skills and knowledge we need to be effective are derived from our experiences in life. Native American society placed great emphasis on eldership because of the experience the elders provided to their tribe. Reverence was given to those who had acquired a great deal of knowledge. Great leaders know how to tap into the experience of their followers. They know that everyone has value regardless of age, gender, or cultural background.

Justice requires the fair and equitable treatment of others. A just person must have unshakable integrity. Being a person of integrity means being guided by a set of moral principles that results in living justly. Those who are unjust, who do not have integrity, will not be accepted by followers. Leaders are responsible for the ethics and norms that pervade their organization. Leaders who are just, set the right moral tone and surround themselves with others who share their values.

Traditionally, we gain *knowledge* through study, research, and the acquisition of skills. Knowledge is gained through familiarity and experience. It is achieved when we become cognizant or conscious of our surroundings and we realize the abundance of learning opportunities. The Native American culture understood that knowledge was inherent in all things. They professed the acquisition of knowledge through listening and waiting. Leaders who value knowledge, create learning organizations where people can contribute all the gifts they have to offer. People will willingly evolve when they work for an organization that values knowledge.

Leadership is a composite of behaviors that can be learned and used by anyone. Many aspects of leadership can be developed in order to effectively interact with others. One of the first steps to becoming a leader is to reflect upon the characteristics you feel a dynamic leader must possess. Native American chiefs were not coercive or authoritarian. They didn't rely on strength or prestige but used fairness, verbal skills, and arbitration to maintain peace and harmony. Their leadership style was one of teaching and facilitation. Those who practice the Native American form of leadership are on a path that will guarantee passionate followers.

Vision suggests a future orientation. It is an ideal image of what we hope to accomplish. To be effective, a vision must be imaginable, obtainable and communicable. Legendary leaders have powerful visions. They also have a mastery of communication, which allows them to provide a common understanding of the vision and the goals needed to bring it to fruition. The visionary leader becomes a catalyst for worthwhile and meaningful transformations.

Reflective thoughts

EARNING THE
HONORED FEATHERS OF
WISDOM

o o o o o o o o o o o o o o o o o o o o o o o o o o o o o o o o o o

"The universe is one great kindergarten for man. Everything that exists has brought with it its own peculiar lesson. The mountain teaches stability and grandeur; the ocean immensity and change. Forests, lakes, and rivers, clouds and winds, stars and flowers, stupendous glaciers and crystal snowflakes, every form of animate or inanimate existence, leaves its impress upon the soul of man. Even the bee and ant have brought their little lessons of industry and economy."

—Orison Swett Marden

ATTRIBUTES OF THE BESTOWER

Compassion

"Try to do something for your people-something difficult. Have pity on your people and love them. If a man is poor, help him. Give him and his family food; give them whatever they ask for. If there is discord among your people, intercede."

—Winnebago lesson

"Tashi would remind me that knowledge and understanding were not sufficient in themselves. In fact they could be dangerous, he would say, if not accompanied with compassion."

—Helene Norberg-Hodge,
Writing about Ladakhi Wisdom

One of the greatest characteristics of any person is the ability to have compassion and mercy for others. Quite often, this characteristic is wrongfully seen as a weakness rather than strength. Native American chiefs constantly strived to meet the needs of every member of the tribe. In fact, if they did not have compassion for others, they wouldn't remain chiefs for very long.

Tecumseh was a chief who was well known for his compassion. He had compassion not only for his tribe but for all those tribes he came in contact with during his many travels. He was also known to have an affinity for the settlers he met. His enemies admired his strength as a warrior, his genius as a leader, his ability as a diplomat, and his compassion for those he defeated in battle.

The attribute of compassion was as evident in Native American cultures as it was in other cultures. Consider the writings of William Shakespeare (1564–1616) who wrote quite eloquently about the importance of compassion in *The Merchant of Venice*. He said, "The quality of mercy is not strained; It droppeth as the gentle rain from heaven," and, "It is enthroned in the hearts of kings."

You can find classes and books galore with the word, "leadership" in the title. They will teach you how to manage, communicate more effectively, be creative, and even balance a budget. Very seldom are we taught how to be more compassionate persons.

For too long, we have left important issues such as compassion to the theologians and philosophers. Business and leadership experts are now writing about mercy and compassion. From all indications, they, and others like them, are having an impact that is long overdue. We need to further explore how we can make mercy and compassion part of our normal business practices.

Certainly there are times when we do not feel at all compassionate towards others. Our endurance can be stretched to the breaking point. Wayne Dyer (1998) in *Wisdom of the Ages*, understands how difficult it can be to show compassion. In his words:

> "As parents, or even adults in positions of authority by virtue of our age and size advantage, we often have the option of displaying our symbols of regal power. It is quite tempting to dole out punishments and to exact revenge when we are disobeyed. Compassion is generally the last thing on our minds…when I am being parental with my children who have broken a rule or failed to live up to an agreement or just generally screwed up in some way, I remember Shakespeare's advice to season justice with mercy."

To offer compassion to those who have in some way offended you or your organization is no easy matter. *Just remember that justice is best served with a side helping of compassion.*

To Native Americans, the rabbit symbolized softness and tenderness. Love, compassion, innocence and trust come to mind when we think about the rabbit. Unfortunately, in today's society, compassion can be seen as being too soft, just like the rabbit. Being a soft, tender, innocent and trusting person can be perceived by some as being ignorant of the way things are in the real world. How sad so many people think this way!

One of the most beloved American generals in history was known for his enduring compassion. Compassion and generalship are terms that are seldom used together. When we think of generals and all things military, the term compassion seldom comes to mind. Yet A.L. Long, in his *Memoirs of Robert E. Lee*, paints a very different picture of what a general can be like:

> "General Lee was visiting a battery on the lines below Richmond, and the soldiers, inspired by their affection for him, gathered near him in a group that attracted the enemy's fire.
>
> "Men, you had better go farther to the rear; they are firing up here, and you are exposing yourselves to unnecessary danger," Lee said.
>
> The men drew back, but Lee, as if unconscious of the danger walked across the yard, picked up some small object from the ground, and placed it upon the limb of a tree above his head. It was afterward perceived that the object for which he had thus risked his life was an unfledged sparrow that had fallen from its nest. It was a marked instance of that love for the lower animals and deep feeling for the helpless which he always displayed."

One of the most moving stories ever written on compassion was by Charles Dickens (1812–1870). All leaders should become familiar with *A Christmas Carol*. It is perhaps one of the best books every written on leadership. Leaders would benefit greatly by familiarizing themselves with the following text that illustrates the importance of compassion:

> "Scrooge fell upon his knees, and clasped his hands before his face.
>
> "Mercy!" he said. "Dreadful apparition, why do you trouble me?"
>
> "Man of the worldly mind!" replied the Ghost, "do you believe in me or not?"
>
> "I do," said Scrooge. "I must. But why do spirits walk the earth, and why do they come to me?"

"It is required of every man," the Ghost returned, "that the spirit within him should walk abroad among his fellowmen, and travel far and wide; and if that spirit goes not forth in life, it is condemned to do so after death. It is doomed to wander through the world-oh, woe is me!-and witness what it cannot share, but might have shared on earth, and turned to happiness!"

Again the spectre raised a cry, and shook its chain and wrung its shadowy hands.

"You are fettered," said Scrooge, trembling. "Tell me why?"

"I wear the chain I forged in life," replied the Ghost. "I made it link by link, and yard by yard; I girded it on of my own free will, and of my own free will I wore it. Is its pattern strange to you?"

Scrooge trembled more and more.

"Or would you know," pursued the Ghost, "the weight and length of the strong coil you bear yourself? It was full, as heavy and as long as this, seven Christmas Eves ago. You have laboured on it, since. It is a ponderous chain!"

Scrooge glanced about him on the floor, in the expectation of finding himself surrounded by some fifty or sixty fathoms of iron cable: but he could see nothing.

"Jacob," he said, imploringly, "Old Jacob Marley, tell me more. Speak comfort to me, Jacob!"

"I have none to give," the Ghost replied. "It comes from other regions, Ebenezer Scrooge, and is conveyed by other ministers, to other kinds of men. Nor can I tell you what I would. A very little more is all permitted to me. I cannot rest, I cannot stay, I cannot linger anywhere. My spirit never walked beyond our counting-house-mark me!-in life my spirit never roved beyond the narrow limits of our money-changing hole; and weary journeys lie before me!"

"Oh! Captive, bound, and double-ironed," cried the phantom, "not to know, that ages of incessant labour by immortal creatures, for this earth must pass into eternity before the good of which t is susceptible is all developed. Not to know that any Christian spirit working kindly in its little sphere, whatever it may be, will find its mortal life too short for its vast means of usefulness. Not to know that no space of regret can make amends for one life's opportunity misused! Yet such was I! Oh! Such was I!"

"But you were always a good man of business, Jacob," faltered Scrooge, who now began to apply this to himself.

"Business!" cried the Ghost, wringing its hands again. "Mankind was my business. The common welfare was my business; charity, mercy, forbearance, and benevolence, were, all, my business. The dealings of my trade were but a drop of water in the comprehensive ocean of my business!"

To have compassion there must be some sense of what others are going through. We must in some way relate to the pain, agony, fear, trepidation, and loss that others are experiencing. We can feel the pain of those who are suffering. We can ask ourselves what we can do to make things better, even for a little while. We can show compassion to those we love and care about and even total strangers.

When I think of compassion shown to others, I am also reminded of a scene from the movie "Saving Private Ryan." In the movie, a woman who works in the War Department during World War II frantically searched through a stack of letters that were being sent to the families of servicemen who had been killed in the war. She had several letters in her hand as she made her way up the Army chain of command.

Eventually, there was a meeting held where it is explained to the Army Chief of Staff that Mrs. Ryan was going to receive three letters on the same day, telling her that three of her four sons had been killed in action. She had only one son left alive and he had been dropped behind enemy lines in France on D-Day.

An impassioned argument ensued about the logic of sending soldiers deep into the war zone to bring Mrs. Ryan's last surviving son safely home. It was during this argument that the Army Chief of Staff brought out an old letter that he read to those gathered in his office. It is obvious that he had read the letter many times. Much of its contents were deeply imbedded in his memory. It said:

"To Mrs. Bixby, Boston, Mass.
Dear Madam,

I have been shown in the files of the War Department a statement of the Adjutant General of Massachusetts that you are the mother of five sons who have died gloriously on the field of battle. I feel how weak and fruitless must be any word of mine which should attempt to beguile you from the grief of a loss so overwhelming. But I cannot refrain from tendering you the consolation that may be found in the thanks of the republic they died to save. I pray that our Heavenly Father may assuage the anguish of your bereavement, and leave you only the cherished memory of the loved and lost, and the solemn pride that must be yours to have laid so costly a sacrifice upon the altar of freedom.

Yours very sincerely and respectfully,

A. Lincoln"

The Army Chief of Staff was experiencing some of the same emotions that Abraham Lincoln experienced when writing to Mrs. Bixby. He had the opportunity to make a decision that might save Mrs. Ryan's only living son. In an act of compassion, he made the decision to bring her son out of the war zone. His decision may not have been a logical one, but it was a compassionate one. Who can say what the outcome will be when we show compassion to others?

The following Ojibway prayer shares the importance that Native American cultures placed on compassion:

We know that in all creation
Only the human family
Has strayed from the Sacred Way.
We know that we are the ones.
Who are divided
And we are the ones
Who must come back together
To walk the Sacred Way.
Grandfather,
Sacred One,
Teach us love, compassion
and honor
That we may heal the earth
And heal each other.

Those who aspired to become chiefs had to show compassion to both followers and enemies. Even while being pursued by the United States cavalry, Chief Joseph showed compassion to every member of his tribe and to the strangers who crossed his path. He was a warrior chief who loved peace and who practiced compassion.

To earn the Honored Feather of Wisdom for compassion:

• Make compassion part of your personal business.

• Spend time assisting a charitable cause you feel strongly about.

• Help out at a local school by tutoring children.

• Be there for someone in need.

Remember and live by the words of Marley's Ghost: "Mankind was my business. The common welfare was my business; charity, mercy, forbearance, and benevolence, were, all, my business. The dealings of my trade were but a drop of water in the comprehensive ocean of my business!"

Reflective thoughts

Kindness

"The public position of the Indian has always been entirely dependent upon our private virtue. We are never permitted to forget that we do not live to ourselves alone, but to our tribe and clan. Every child, from the first days of learning, is a public servant in training…in this way, children were shown that big-heartedness, generosity, courage, and self-denial are the qualifications of a public servant, and from the cradle we sought to follow this ideal."

—Ohiyesa

"A good heart and a good mind—these are what you need to be a chief."

—Louis Farmer,
Onondaga Elder

Great leaders use their hearts and minds when making decisions and interacting with others. Leaders who do not have a heart will lack the followers they need to be effective. People only follow tyrants out of fear. Leaders such as Sitting Bull understood that kindness helped secure a position of leadership. Sitting Bull was part of a culture where the values of kindness and generosity were greatly valued and practiced by their leaders.

The Sioux, like other Native Americans, believed in kindness and generosity. The accumulation of property for its own sake was an unacceptable and disdained practice. Status was awarded based upon what one gave away to the less fortunate, not upon how much one could accumulate.

Sitting Bull abolished slavery in his own tribe and extended compassion to captives of war. He ordered the members of his tribe to either adopt or release those who had been captured and enslaved during their wars. He also gave his earnings from the Buffalo Bill tour to poor white children. He didn't understand how a rich society could mistreat those less fortunate.

Sitting Bulls father, Jumping Bull, was killed at a battle between his people, the Hunkpapas, and the Crow. The Crow were killed in retaliation and while returning to camp, Sitting Bull found three Crow women and a baby who had been left behind by the defeated enemies. Sitting Bull did not allow his tribesmen to kill these captives. Rather, he gave them horses and released them. Although grieved by the loss of his father, he understood that the captives also grieved the loss of their tribesmen. To act any other way would have been disrespectful to the memory of his father.

Similar acts of kindness are also seen in our military operations today. The role of our military has taken on a new dimension that goes beyond war fighting capability. Our men and women in uniform have taken on the task of peacekeepers. Not only does our military defend America's freedom, they also shelter homeless, feed hungry, and protect defenseless people around the world.

Cheryl Dahle (2000) says preserving a culture of kindness is a full-time job at a company called *Play* in Richmond, Virginia. The company "ambassador" is also the keeper of the internal flame. She does this with small gestures that reflect her commitment to others.

"I'll ask different people for their car keys, and then I'll go fill up their car with gas and wash it," she says. "I place a plastic cone in front of the building and reserve it for a certain person for the day. When somebody goes on a road trip, we put water and fruit in a bag and hand it to that person on the way out the door. The other day, I bought 31 milk shakes and brought them in. You would have thought I brought in a million dollars. It was just $80 worth of milk shakes.

What's 80 bucks in the grand scheme of things when it comes to keeping people excited about being here?"

In 1996, a *U.S. News & World Report* survey found that 88 percent of Americans thought incivility was a serious problem. Respondents to the survey cited the consequences of incivility to be eroding moral values, divided communities, and an increase in violence. Respondents to the survey were all too eager to point their finger at others as the reason for the loss of civility. Only one percent of those surveyed admitted to being uncivil, the other 99 percent blamed others.

Since that report, a more recent news poll found that 11 percent of Americans say they've made an obscene gesture at another driver in the last few months and 42 percent admitted to swearing in public. Recently, I quickly exited a store with my family in tow after hearing someone verbally "pealing the paint" off the wall in a video rental store because they didn't have the videotape he wanted. I suppose I could have explained the importance of civility to the paint peeler. I could have explained that there were children in the store and that his behavior was not appreciated. But in today's society, angry drivers are shooting people on highways. High school students are killing other students because they felt they had been slighted in the past.

There are numerous tales concerning incivility in the workplace. Many of them deal with little nuisances such as refusing to refill the coffee pot when you've taken the last cup, using the last of the paper in the copier and not refilling it or leaving it jammed. Sometimes the incivility centers on issues of rudeness such as unkind words or having a dismissive attitude toward others.

Lee (1998) cites Christine Pearson, a management professor at the University of North Carolina, who conducted a four-year study of rudeness, insensitivity and disrespect in the workplace. She asked 775 respondents to describe an unpleasant interaction in which they were the targets of bullying-receiving a nasty note, being accused of a lack of knowledge, being shouted at and how they responded. Most people retaliate against their employers rather than the instigator. She found 28 percent lost work time avoiding the person; 22 percent decreased their effort at work; 10 percent decreased the amount of time they spent at work; and 12 percent changed jobs to avoid the instigator.

Jamie Sams (1998) explains:

> "If, for instance, we could see the energy connected to hurtful words as they tear through our energy fields, and if we could watch the diminishing of our life force as the verbal blow is received, we would never scream at or taunt another person. Harsh or cruel words aimed at another can create the same damage that a weapon creates when used violently on the body…Indigenous

tribal cultures worldwide practice forms of etiquette that are as individual and diverse as the tribes themselves. One thread running through many tribes is the practice of speaking no harm. The habit of working in silence or singing while at work and using storytelling to fill the community's need to come together in groups and communicate leave no room for careless, hurtful words or gossip. The understanding that all words reflect and create positive or negative energy in the unseen worlds keep negative chatter from bringing discord into daily life. By using silence as a way of being, tribal people are given access to clear minds, which allow energy to be seen. Other worlds existing within nature are open to them through this silence, and consequently there is more harmony within the tribe. When energy is not leaked through negativity, boundless inspiration is available for creating dance, stories, and ceremonies that celebrate every individual's role as a cherished member of the tribe."

Kindness is a key attribute that leads to wisdom. The myths and stories we want to create about ourselves and our organization should be of kindness. To earn the Honored Feather of Wisdom for kindness:

- If you hear others denigrating someone, mention something nice about that person.

- Be thoughtful in your comments to and about others.

- Never pass up an opportunity to do some act of kindness for another.

- If you see someone doing something right, let him or her know you appreciate it.

- Speak no harm.

Reflective thoughts

Patience

"Our white relatives say the Indian is stoic. This is not necessarily true. We just wait to see the true person. Given time, he will show his true self, so wait and time will provide the proof."

—Phil Lane, Sr.,
Yankton Lakota Elder

Is patience a virtue? How do we treat those who take time to ponder the really big issues, the jugular issues? Do you really want the boss to take extra time to make a decision on something you feel passionate about? Do you want to take the extra time? If you read the latest business literature, you see that speed gets a lot more press than patience as a characteristic to be emulated by the up-and-coming.

In today's society we evaluate performance based upon what we've accomplished in the last few minutes, hours, or days. Patience is seen as something we do not have time for. When was the last time you received a pat on the back because you took additional time to assess a project, task, or individual? How many times have we suffered because we had to fill a vacant position immediately and didn't take the time to find out that our new team player couldn't spell "team", much less be on one. The way we do business would drastically change if patience were truly seen as an attribute of wisdom.

Certainly we are living in a time where speed is of the essence. Competition is a real issue for any business. But patience is seen as a weakness rather than strength. Some people go so far as to attack others verbally and physically when they do not reach an immediate agreement.

Recent studies show that we tend to admire those who demean and belittle others. We admire an impressive vocabulary, smart-talk, more than content. Those who are good at putting others down are more likely to advance their careers than those who don't. It is often too late that we recognize someone was all talk and no substance. Patience may be a virtue, but having it can be hazardous to your career.

Professor and author Henry Mintzberg (1975) examined the effect of multiple demands on managers by studying how managers actually work. He discovered that managers were perceived as reflective, methodical planners with time to systematically plan and work through their day. In reality, typical managers take on so much and encounter such constant interruption that little time remains for reflection. Events range from trivialities to crises; the average time spent on one activity is only nine minutes.

Since managers are so tapped for time, is it any wonder that more than two-thirds of change efforts fail? Wheatley (1997) explains that over the years, managers have opted for control rather than productivity in the workplace. Organizations are cluttered with control mechanisms that bring about organizational paralysis.

It takes patience to bring about meaningful and lasting change. Wheatley states, "If we've learned anything in the past 20 years, it's that there are no quick fixes.

For most organizations, meaningful change is at least a three-to five-year process-although this seems impossibly long for managers."

We lack the patience it takes to move away from our old Industrial Age based business models. Wheatley correctly points out that Motorola has struggled with their quality control program. Jack Welch, CEO, understood it would take at least 10 years to develop the capacities of General Electric's people.

How is it within your organization? How many supposedly sacrosanct programs have gone away when we discovered we didn't have the commitment or the patience to see them through? We need to rethink the importance of patience and the positive-impact that attribute can have on each of our organizations and us.

When thinking of patience, think of nature and her seasons and how they change ever so gradually. The blooming of flowers each spring is a metaphor for the concept of patience. After a long and cold winter you can see the stalks of flowers sprouting their colorful and fragrant blooms. It is as though they have somehow synchronized their rebirth in order to delight anyone who is willing to wait and watch with patience.

Flowers are a part of the story of humanity. They are woven into the very fabric of every religion, mythology, and folklore. They are used in celebrations and to express feelings. They are used to heal us physically and emotionally.

The iris is special to me just as it was to my ancestors. In ancient times, it was believed that the goddess Iris was the messenger of the gods and the personification of the rainbow. Just as the goddess Iris carefully conveyed the words of the gods, we should weigh our words before we speak. Thoughtfully speaking our thoughts is a form of patience that is not often practiced. Just as Iris symbolizes the rainbow, our patience is best expressed after we have reflected upon the rain that has fallen on our lives. The rainbow comes after the storm, not before it.

How many times have we wished to take back a word uttered in haste? How many times has a brief storm caused irreversible damage? We are left with hurt feelings and hurt lives.

Patience is an attribute of wisdom that was commonly practiced throughout the Native American culture. Patience was possible because the people were trained when they were children to patiently listen and reflect upon everything around them. That included the words of their elders, and the sounds of nature, plants and animals. With patience and reflective thought, answers would come in time.

"If we're looking for truth about our people, it's not in the textbooks and it's not anywhere where we can pop it up on a computer, the way the white man's education wants us to do-the white system wants us to hurry up and find something and read it and go take a test and pass it and, suddenly, you know it and you're smart. When we were growing up, we were taught that you don't ask questions. You just have to stay around and listen and the answer will come to you. Just keep thinking about it, and you'll get your answer. And we weren't told a lot of things because at the time it was felt we couldn't under-stand it-couldn't understand the answers. Eventually, all the answers you need come to you. We are now living in an impatient society that doesn't allow for this process-we have to go to the library or call information so we can have our answers immediately. We're always in a hurry."

—Linda Poolaw,
All Roads are Good

Ohiyesa believed silence to be the cornerstone of character. He also identified the truths of silence as being: self-control, true courage or endurance, patience, dignity, and reverence. He had the following to say about his fellow Native Americans:

"He believes profoundly in silence-the sign of a perfect equilibrium. Silence is the absolute poise or balance of body, mind, and spirit. The man who pre-serves his selfhood ever calm and unshaken by the storms of existence-not a leaf, as it were, astir on the tree, not a ripple upon the surface of the shining pool-his, in the mind of the unlettered sage, is the ideal attitude and conduct of life…
    Silence is the cornerstone of character."

Chief Wabasha and Ohiyesa shared the same respect for the value of silence. Chief Wabasha said that you must guard your tongue in youth and in age so that you may mature a thought that will be of service to your people. His words would be hailed as nuggets of wisdom in many boardrooms where enormous amounts of time are wasted in useless breast-beating and showmanship.

Can you imagine the good work that could be accomplished if time was set aside for silent reflection on issues such as core values, key organizational indica-tors and mission essential goals? More organizations now understand the impor-tance of reflective thinking and its benefits. We are also discovering that there is an integral link between reflective thinking and natural settings.

Chief Seattle, a Suqwamish and Duwamish leader gave an interesting perspec-tive on the importance of nature and silence:

"The sight of your cities pains the eyes of the red man. But perhaps it is because the red man is a savage and does not understand.

There is no quiet place in the white man's cities, no place to hear the leaves of spring or the rustle of insects' wings. Perhaps it is because I am a savage and do not understand, but the clatter only seems to insult the ears.

The Indian prefers the soft sound of the wind darting over the face of the pond, the smell of the wind itself cleansed by the midday rain, or scented with pine. The air is precious to the red man, for all things share the same breath-the animals, the trees, the man."

Native Americans understood the value of patience. They were taught how to be patient when they were children and they continued along that path throughout their lives. Those who misunderstood their reflective nature saw great chiefs as stoic. Time was measured by the seasons, not by a watch synchronized with the atomic clock. They weighed their words thoughtfully before they spoke, and when they spoke, they meant exactly what they said.

Tho earn the Honored Feather of Wisdom for patience:

- Treat patience as a virtue, not as a weakness.

- Think before you speak. Words uttered in haste are irreversible.

- Listen to what others are saying with all your senses.

- Set aside time regularly for silent reflective thinking.

- Take time to listen to the sounds of nature.

Reflective thoughts

Respect

"Children were taught that true politeness was to be defined in actions rather than in words. Children were not allowed to pass between the fire and an older person or a visitor, to speak while others were speaking, or to make fun of a handicapped or disfigured person. If a child thoughtlessly tried to do so, a parent, in a quiet voice, immediately set them straight."

—Chief Luther Standing Bear,
Teton Sioux

Respect, in Native American culture, manifested itself in the way the elderly were treated and the respect they were shown. According to Beck, Walters and Francisco (1977), the status of the aged in North American tribes was one of honor and respect because having lived long entitled both men and women to certain privileges that were not extended to other members of the tribe.

"If you are good to old people, these in turn will pray to the Supreme Being for your health, long life, and success. Children were instructed explicitly to be good to the aged, to feed them, to clothe and to help them in difficulties, as well as to seek out those so blessed and ask for their prayers."

Among all tribes, elderly people had certain rights. They could give advice, lecture and counsel younger people. They go on to say:

> "Whether the advice or counseling was heeded or not was another matter. But it was the right of elderly people to make their opinions known. Often elderly people held positions of authority in the household and in the ceremonial life of the tribe. Older people often speak of their age and what it means in terms of life's cycle."

Just as Native Americans respected the elderly, many businesses are beginning to respect the contributions of older Americans. Today, one in every nine Americans is 65 or older. It is estimated that by the year 2030, the statistic will reflect one in five. Although Congress has prohibited mandatory retirement, many companies still ignore indisputable trends. Organizations that are conscious of the potential of the elderly are going to reap rewards.

We respect what we value. In our society we often value material objects. Unfortunately, we sometimes do a lousy job of valuing others. *Quite often we fail to see the value of those we come in contact with.* And as a society, we have failed to value the elderly in the same way the Native Americans valued their elders.

Many of us were raised to be respectful of others. Some might argue that the benefit of learning to be respectful of others was for those who were being shown respect. The real benefit of those early lessons was personal development.

The benefit of being taught to honor and respect others is in learning the value of others. We may not know why someone is special, just that they are, and since they are special they should be treated with respect. This was certainly true in the Native American culture and is lacking in our culture today.

In today's business world, the closest we come to respecting and honoring others is in issues of diversity and mentorship. The value of diversity lies in the theory that a broad scope of ideas is critical to organizational survival. Therefore, we look for those who are different than we are because, after all, if they are different they may see things differently. If I treat those unlike me with respect, they may feel comfortable enough to come up with new ideas to generate revenue. This is not exactly a noble reason for appreciating diversity but it is a move in the right direction.

FedEx has made "respect for others" one of their nine criteria for identifying potential leaders. Respect for others at FedEx is seen as honoring and not belittling the opinions or work of other people, regardless of their status or position.

Leaders no longer manage a homogeneous work force. People in present day organizations represent a kaleidoscope of diversity in age, race, culture and ethnicity. They must also deal with full time, part time and temporary employees. These people best contribute physical and intellectual capital to our organizations when their diversity is respected. One way to ensure they contribute is to establish a mentorship program which values diversity.

Mentoring dates back to Greek mythology when Odysseus departed for the Trojan War and charged his household manager, Mentor, with the task of educating and guiding his son. Mentor acted as a teacher, coach, taskmaster, confidant, counselor and friend to Odysseus' son. The role of mentoring has persisted throughout history and has gained popularity in business over the last few years.

Today, mentorship appears to be most commonly associated with performance improvement. The mentees respects the mentors because they have valuable knowledge or skill that will improve their performance and thus give them an edge over the competition. This isn't all bad; who wouldn't want to hone their skills or beat out the competition? This is the latter-day version of sitting at the master's feet. But rather than being the holy person of old, the master is a very skilled salesperson, marketer, computer wizard or politician.

What appears to be missing today isn't really respect because we respect others for reasons such as: having knowledge, a nasty temper, positional power, or financial security.

What appears to be missing from the equation is respecting others because it is the right thing to do. It's easy to respect others because you see them being better than you are, because they have some attribute you'd like to possess, or because you fear them. Where is the challenge in that? The real challenge is in respecting others because it is the right thing to do and, in showing respect to others, you'll become a better person. General William Harrison shared his respect for Tecumseh as follows:

> "The implicit obedience and respect which followers of Tecumseh pay him is really astonishing and more than any other circumstance bespeaks him one of

those uncommon geniuses which spring up occasionally to produce revolutions and overturn the established order of things. If it were not for the vicinity of the United States, he would perhaps be the founder of an Empire that would rival in glory Mexico or Peru."

Giving Honor, a first cousin of respect, is the practice of taking time to publicly recognize the accomplishments of others. It is complimenting someone for doing good to others. I really like the idea of giving honor to others. It is a great way to show reverence to those who have given of themselves for the benefit of others.

Reverence is having profound awe, respect and love for others. From time to time it is necessary to ask questions about reverence. These questions are: Who do you revere? Why do you revere them? What have you done to let them know that you are aware of their accomplishments?

By giving honor to others we send the message that we are aware of them and what they do. We should let people know they are noticed, appreciated and contributing to the organization. By giving honor we send a message, loud and clear, that it is good to honor others for their works.

Unfortunately, there are many organizations that have created a culture of finger pointing and faultfinding. This can be labeled as giving dishonor. This rancorous way of dealing with others brings only dissonance and hostility into organizations. Why would anyone start a meeting by finding fault with others?

"I can't believe what happened in Joe's section last week, what a bunch of losers," or "Let me tell you how bad one of our sections messed up last week." This isn't a formula for successful group interaction.

Of course there are times and places where we need to address opportunities for performance improvement. These opportunities should be handled privately, not as a public execution. Deriding others in public is mean-spirited and unworthy of thoughtful leadership.

We should strive to be the catalyst that brings consonance and harmony to our organization. If you've asked yourself the questions listed above, the next step is to show reverence to those who truly deserve it. At your next meeting or public event, take time to give honor and respect to someone who is deserving. You'll have made an important contribution that will pay dividends to you and those you are honoring, now and in the future.

We should remember that great leaders were revered by their followers because they revered others. General Robert E. Lee was one of these leaders. His military achievements may have been rivaled or even surpassed by other military leaders, but none of the other commanders were loved by their followers the way General Lee was.

Holton (1999) shares with his readers the comments of Colonel Withers in A.L. Long's *Memoirs of Robert E. Lee*:

> "But General Lee never forgot that his men were fellow-beings as well as soldiers. He cared for them with parental solicitude, nor ever relaxed in his efforts to promote their comfort and protect their lives."

In those same memoirs, it was said that General Lee was never heard to speak disparagingly of anyone, and when anyone was heard so to speak in his presence he would always recall some trait of excellence in the absent one.

How could you not respect someone who was always looking out for your welfare and refused to speak disparagingly of you and others? These were acts that embody the very essence of respect and reverence.

According to Anne Wilson Schaef (1995) it was Irish writer Daniel Martin who stated the following:

> "The associated attributes [of the Celtic warrior mentality] illustrates this particular understanding [that warriors were agents of change]: respect, awareness of fear, wakefulness, and self-confidence."

Schaef feels that respect is not a common commodity in our modern world; *fear and awe are very common but respect is a rarity*. She points out that the Celtic warrior was a great example of the type of person who would be held in high esteem in other tribal groups. Such a warrior had respect for all members of the tribe. Native American warriors received and gave this same type of respect within their tribe.

Chief Luther Standing Bear and the ancient Celtic warriors knew that respect was one of many attributes that needed to be learned before a person achieved true wisdom. They also knew that respect is best defined by action rather than words. There is an old Arapaho proverb that says, "When we show our respect for other living things, they respond with respect for us."

To earn the Honored Feather of Wisdom for respect:

- Always remember that true politeness is defined in actions rather than words.

- Deal with the impoliteness of others in a quiet voice.

- Everyone has value, so respect the uniqueness of others.

- Honor the opinion of others regardless of their status.

Reflective thoughts

Sacrifice

"Take your sacred pipe and walk into their midst. Die if necessary in your attempt to bring about reconciliation. Then, when order has been restored and they see you lying dead on the ground, still holding in your hand the sacred pipe, the symbol of peace and reconciliation, then assuredly will they know that you have been a real chief."

—Winnebago lesson

"The higher the level of leadership you want to reach, the greater the sacrifices you will have to make. To go up, you have to give up. That is the true nature of leadership. That is the Law of Sacrifice."

—John C. Maxwell, *The 21 Irrefutable Laws of Leadership*

Sacrifice can entail many different things. Sacrifice can be as simple an act as turning off the television or the computer in order to play a game with a child. It can mean giving up an hour, a day, or several days to help someone.

We sacrifice ourselves for many different reasons. Putting in extra hours at work to make enough money for ourselves and our loved ones is a sacrifice. We may give up family time to earn a degree that will help us in the future. Some people donate a pint of blood to the Red Cross to help those in need. Despite the vehicle, we hope our small sacrifices might make a difference to someone.

People have been known to sacrifice their time, money, relationships, ideas, health, freedom, and even their lives.

Henry Taylor said, "He who gives what he would as readily throw away, gives without generosity; for the essence of generosity is in self-sacrifice."

Kristen Maree Cleary (1996) explains that the values and beliefs held by many of the five hundred Native American nations have endured and reemerged as a testament to the unshakable tenacity even in the face of overwhelming sacrifice.

"Stories of the courage, defiance, and wisdom of tribal elders, holy people, warriors, and wise women have been passed down through the ages, providing inspiration to successive generations."

They didn't know it then, but the sacrifices they made for their families had a ripple effect that is felt to this day. What they did for others is not unlike the story told in the holiday classic, *It's a Wonderful Life*. In that story, the main character, George Balley, played by Jimmy Stewart, temporarily gave up his plans to go to college in order to save the family business after his father's death, and to put his brother through college. Four years later when his brother returned from college with a new bride and a promising career opportunity, he once again opted to sacrifice his own dreams in order to help someone else.

Whenever he came close to realizing his personal dreams, fate would step in and his hopes would be dashed. Somehow he persevered for years, even though the path he found himself on was not the one he imagined. In his youth, George had dreams to "lasso the moon." Instead he assumed a position of responsibility within his community where he could help others.

It took a financial calamity to drive him to the brink of suicide. After having sacrificed his dreams for many years, all of his hard work and sacrifice was about to be lost. He envisioned being humiliated, disgraced, and even imprisoned for a careless act that was not his fault. In a deep state of depression he mistakenly decided that the only solution to his problem was to take his own life. He couldn't see the good he had done. He could only see the bad.

Just in time, a guardian angel named Clarence Oddbody appeared. Clarence was on a mission to save George and to earn his wings in the process. He showed George what the world would be like if he hadn't been born. In retrospect, George realized he had saved his brother from drowning when they were very young, even though it cost George his hearing in one ear. He had saved other lives when, as a young man, he challenged a prescription that had been erroneously filled by a grieving pharmacist whose son had just died of influenza. His wonderful marriage and beautiful family would never have existed. And his long time business rival, Mr. Potter, would have destroyed the decent community that George had come to know and love.

It wasn't until Clarence showed him all this that he realized that his life, and all the sacrifices he had made, were purposeful. His life was wonderful because he had made it so. His wonderful life was possible because of his generous nature and willingness to put the needs of others ahead of his own. His positive impact was made apparent when the town rallied behind him and rushed to his house to offer assistance. His sacrifices brought him the love and respect of his family, friends, and the community he had served all of his life.

Just like George Balley, we often think of sacrifice as being something that is done by others, not by us. *Sacrifice is seen too often as an extreme act.* Sacrifice is sometimes misunderstood as involving only an extreme act such as giving ones life to protect country and freedom. This, of course, is the ultimate form of sacrifice and we rightfully honor those who give everything they have for what they believe in.

It was Grenville Kleiser who succinctly said:

> "There are fine things, which you mean to do some day, under what you think will be more favorable circumstances. But the only time that is surely yours is the present, hence this is the time to speak the word of appreciation and sympathy, to do the generous deed, to forgive the fault of a thoughtless friend, to sacrifice self a little more for others. Today is the day in which to express your noblest qualities of mind and heart, to do at least one worthy thing which you have long postponed, and to use your God-given abilities for the enrichment of someone less fortunate. Today you can make your life significant and worthwhile. The present is yours to do with as you will."

Most people make sacrifices; we just don't dwell upon them or truly understand the effect they have. Our sacrifices literally take on their own life. But unlike George Balley, we don't have a Clarence Oddbody helping us see exactly how much our sacrifices have influenced others. Just trust that a good deed is always rewarded, even when the reward is not immediately apparent.

John C. Maxwell (1998) said, "you have to give up in order to go up." He emphasized that many people today want to climb up the corporate ladder because they see freedom and power as the prizes that await them. They don't truly realize that sacrifice is deeply etched into the other side of the leadership coin.

You don't have to be the president of the United States or the CEO of a Fortune 500 corporation to realize the truth in Maxwell's profound words. There are many great individuals who come to mind when we think of sacrifice. Maxwell cites Martin Luther King Jr. as someone who sacrificed it all while pursuing his course of leadership:

> "King was arrested and jailed on many occasions. He was stoned, stabbed, and physically attacked. His house was bombed. Yet his vision-and his influence-continued to increase. Ultimately, he sacrificed everything he had."

Dr. King willingly sacrificed himself even though he desired life. He openly expressed his commitment to do God's will. He acted upon his vision of a future Promised Land. His vision brought him happiness and dispelled his fear of those who would do him harm.

Our greatest heroes understood the need to sacrifice of themselves. Dr. King understood; so did Crazy Horse, Tecumseh, Chief Joseph, and many others.

Kristen Maree Cleary (1996) explains the magnitude of sacrifice experienced by Native Americans.

> "During the five hundred years since the arrival of the first European colonists, Native Americans have seen the beloved, hallowed earth of Turtle Island—name used by some tribes for America-invaded, appropriated, deforested, and polluted. Dispossessed of their homelands, removed far from the territories that sustained their lifeways, many of the first peoples were devastated by disease and warfare. Those who survived were forced to accept new ways, to learn another's language, schooled in a religion unknown to them, and forbidden to practice traditional sacred rites."

In the end, many of our leaders and their followers experienced very unpleasant, even fatal repercussions. Yet the sacrifices they made stand as lessons for us to emulate. Sacrificing oneself for the benefit of others is the noblest of acts.

To earn the Honored Feather of Wisdom for sacrifice:

- Take every opportunity to bring about reconciliation whenever and wherever it is needed.

- Be cognizant of the sacrifices made by others and acknowledge their good works.

- Don't expect to know what impact your sacrifices will have on others. Just be confident that your sacrifices will be rewarded.

- There is no time like the present to make a sacrifice for the benefit of others. What sacrifices can you make right now that will make a difference to others?

Reflective thoughts

Sharing

"It has always been our belief that the love of possessions is a weakness to be overcome. Its appeal is to the material part, and if allowed its way it will in time disturb the spiritual balance for which we all strive. Therefore we must early learn the beauty of generosity. As children we are taught to give what we prize most, that we may taste the happiness of giving; at an early age we are made the family giver of alms. If a child is inclined to be grasping, or to cling too strongly to possessions, legends are related that tell of the contempt and disgrace falling on those who are ungenerous and mean."

—Ohiyesa

"I am a big man. See all these shells? They are very valuable in our culture. I could have trunks of them...but then I wouldn't be a big man. A big man gives away what he has and shares with others."

—New Guinea Elder

"It is a strict law that bids us distribute our property among our friends and neighbors. It is a good law."

—Kwakiutl, 1886

Sharing comes easier to some people than it does to others. For example, holidays bring out the best in many of us as we take time to reflect on life's many blessings and share those blessings with others. For some the act of sharing comes naturally and consistently; for others the act appears to be forced and seasonal.

The Native American concept of sharing was a timeless concept that many would be wise to adopt. Ohiyesa, explained that the true Native American sets no price upon either his property or his labor.

"Generosity was only limited by the strength and ability of the giver. It was an honor to be selected for a difficult or dangerous task. It would have been shameful to ask for any reward. It was believed that the person being served would express their thanks according to their own bringing up and their sense of honor."

Today we sometimes see the right person step forward and share their talent in order to meet the needs of their organization. Many times the reward for sharing ones talent is financial, at other times it is emotional. A combination of both, appeals to most of us. Great leaders discover those who are shy about sharing their talents, nurture them, and assist them to benefit the entire organization.

Another way to look at the concept of sharing was explained by Maquinna, a Nootka Chief. He said he saw a very large house. He was told that the house was actually a bank. To his amazement, he was told that a bank is where men put their money so the money can be taken care of and eventually, they get their money back with interest. Maquinna explained the following:

> "We are Indians and we have no such bank; but when we have plenty of money or blankets, we give them away to other chiefs and people, and by and by they return them with interest, and our hearts feel good. Our way of giving is our bank."

A Sauk named Black Hawk shared this same sentiment:

> "Throughout our lives we must do what we conceive to be good. If we have corn and meat, and know of a family that has none, we divide with them. If we have more blankets than are sufficient, and others have not enough, we must give to them that want."

Sharing is both good for the giver and the receiver. Studies have shown that leaders who openly share with others tend to gain greater respect from their subordinates. *The willingness to share with others adds humanness to one's persona.*

The French anthropologist Pierre Clastres (1977) explains that an important characteristic of an Indian Chief is his generosity. Such sharing is both a duty and bondage. Clastres quotes Francis Huxley on practices of the Urubu people: "It is the business of a chief to be generous and to give what is asked of him. In some Indian tribes you can always tell the chief because he has the fewest possessions and wears the shabbiest ornaments. He has had to give away everything else."

One of the finest examples of sharing I've observed was not experienced in the workplace but, rather, at home. The one person in my life who has shown me the value and the joy of sharing is my wife. Cindy has always been the type of person who shares with others, and for all the right reasons.

I've never known her to have a personal agenda associated with the act of sharing. This might be called "unconditional sharing." The gifts she most often gives are her time and her talent. Her sharing is visibly present at our children's schools, the church, the community, and amongst family, friends, and strangers.

Through watching her I have learned that sharing is more than throwing a few coins into the Salvation Army bucket when hurriedly walking into or away from a store. It goes far beyond filling out an annual pledge card for a deserving charity. Sharing is giving of whatever resources or talent you are lucky enough to have in order to help others.

For some this might be accomplished by teaching a course. For others it may be sharing a special talent with someone. It can be as simple as offering someone food or clothing. Sharing can be as complicated as a heart-to-heart discussion that you know you need to have with someone you care about.

The attribute of sharing was deeply prized amongst Native Americans. They knew that in order to be wise, a chieftain must first be a person who understood the importance of sharing. Greed and selfishness were considered serious crimes in many native cultures and were severely punished. We tend to frown upon greed and selfishness in Western culture while tacitly accepting and in some cases admiring these attributes.

Anita Roddick (1991), CEO of "The Body Shop," broke all the rules of what a business should be. She saw modern business as being immoral. She despised the common business environment in which greed was respectable and worth was measured by the accumulation of wealth. In her words:

> "I am mystified by the fact that the business world is apparently proud to be seen as hard and uncaring and detached from human values. Why is altruism in business seen as alien to the point where anyone claiming to be motivated by it is considered suspect? I personally don't know how the hell anybody can survive running a successful business in the nineties without caring. I don't

know how they keep their role within the community. I don't know how they keep their soul intact. There is not even any humanity in business language."

Sadly, Anita Roddick was very much in the minority when she entered the business arena. Terms such as sharing and caring are synonymous with her creation of her very successful business, "The Body Shop." According to her, business practices would improve immeasurably if they were guided by feminine principles such as love, care, and intuition. Her principles would likely agree with the precept of Clara Honea, an Athabaskan elder:

"They always told us to share food, even if it's our last.

Never let anyone leave our home without a meal.

Never make bad feelings over food,

because food comes along every day."

Chiefs of the Chinook, Nootka, and other Pacific Northwest Native American tribes vied to give the most blankets and other valuables to others. In hunter-gatherer societies, the hunter's status was not determined by how much of the kill he ate or stored for his own use, but rather by what he brought back for others to eat.

This is similar to the field of science where the scientist with the highest status is not the one who possesses the most knowledge, but the one who has contributed the most to the field. A scientist with great knowledge, but only minor contributions, is unlikely to be held in the same esteem as someone who is making more contributions to the field.

"Always assume your guest is tired, cold, and hungry, and act accordingly. Even as you desire good treatment, so render it. Who serves his fellows is of all the greatest. If you see no reason for giving thanks, the fault lies in yourself."

—Native American Proverb

In his book, *The Gift*, Lewis Hyde tells the story of early interactions between the Native Americans and the Pilgrims. The Native Americans brought a fine peace pipe to this first meeting and gave it to the Pilgrims. According to Hyde, the Pilgrims began to think of sending it back to the British Museum to be displayed. These early settlers were surprised when the Native Americans came back expecting to smoke from the pipe and have the pipe returned to them. The Pilgrims thought that once a gift was given it became their property. The Native Americans believed that a gift must move.

Obviously, there were serious differences in how Native Americans and the Pilgrims viewed property. The Pilgrims saw goods as something you possessed. The Native Americans like other indigenous cultures, saw most possessions as part of a common flow.

I received a phone call from a close friend in mid-December, 1999. He asked if I would be in my office for a while because he wanted to see me. As he stepped into my office, I noticed two things. The first was an immense smile that told me he was very pleased to be with me and that he was also very proud of something. The second thing I noticed was a beautiful "talking stick," ornately decorated with feathers, beads, and rawhide.

He explained that he had enjoyed many of the articles I had written, especially the ones about the use of a talking stick when entering into group dialogue. He made this talking stick from a sassafras root. A vine had grown around the root and made a deeply embedded curving line that repeatedly circled around the entire length of the root. He used rawhide to connect beads and other ornaments to the stick. It was obvious from the detailed work on the talking stick that he had spent hours working on this wonderful gift. He handed me a Christmas card with a personalized note inside that read, "For my friend and mentor...many times I've heard you mention the tribal custom of the 'talking stick.' Merry Christmas my friend, use it, don't display it!"

I have used the talking stick on several occasions. It is a reminder of a generous act, of friendship, and the importance of dialogue. It is a work in progress. I have personalized the talking stick, just as my friend wanted me too. His act of generosity was very much in alignment with the Native American concept of sharing.

To earn an Honored Feather of Wisdom for sharing:

- Give away what you prize most so that you may learn the beauty of generosity.

- Take on difficult tasks that stretch your ability to the limit. Do this without thought of reward.

- Give generously to those who have need.

- Donate your time and money to a charitable cause.

Reflective thoughts

ATTRIBUTES OF THE COMPANION

Appreciation

"A man's deeds were also recited and proclaimed both by himself and his supporters at virtually every opportunity. His claim to fame was through the acquisition of honors, by which he gradually rose in status and these, when combined with other qualities such as generosity, skills in diplomacy, and so forth, might lead to election to chieftainship."

—Norman Bancroft-Hunt,
Warriors: Warfare and the Native American Indian

John Adams, 2nd US President, said, "A desire to be observed, considered, esteemed, praised, beloved, and admired by his fellows is one of the earliest as well as keenest dispositions discovered in the heart of man."

Praise and recognition is how we show appreciation to others.

In Native American societies one important and customary way to recognize the accomplishments of others was through the giving of an eagle feather. The conferring of an eagle feather was a sacred act; as such, prayers and songs were part of the ritual that accompanied the receipt of the feather.

Praise and recognition were given in Native American cultures for a variety of reasons such as having worked hard, provided for the tribe, or served bravely as a warrior. *Feathers were earned by helping the people of the tribe.*

In organizations today, people are usually not overly deluged with accolades from their boss or co-workers. How many bosses greet their employees each morning with a pat on the back while telling them what a fantastic job they've done for the organization? Yet, there is something inside each of us that craves that type of attention.

Realistically, we don't expect bosses or co-workers to greet us each morning with a cup of coffee and effusive praise. A simple "thank you" will far exceed most people's expectations When an adult breaks down in tears after being recognized for the very first time after many years of devoted service, you begin to understand how important it is to show appreciation. It's sad that so few people get recognized for the good work they do within their organizations.

Is it any wonder many people take on the characteristics of the tortoise after having been ignored for years of dutiful service? What are the characteristics of the tortoise? One of the characteristics is becoming over protective of oneself. They don't want their feelings to become hurt so they downplay their contributions. Rather than opening up to others they become withdrawn. Just like the tortoise, when they feel they are under too much pressure and under-appreciated, they will also snap at others. How is it where you work? Are you surrounded by people who have put on a protective shell? Are people snapping at each other? This may be an indication that people do not feel appreciated for their efforts.

Showing appreciation is one of the smartest and easiest things you can do. Leaders should show appreciation in a timely manner. Leaders must be observant and show appreciation whenever and wherever the opportunity arises. If not, we are liable to lose the very people we need most.

Bob Nelson (1994), in his book *1001 Ways to Reward Employees* cites Ken Blanchard who said:

"If there's one thing I've learned in my life, it's the fact that everyone wants to be appreciated. This goes for managers as well as employees, parents as well as children, and coaches as well as players. We never outgrow this need and even if it looks like we are independent and self-sufficient, the fact is we need others to help us feel valued. Although this might sound like common sense, so often I've found that common sense is not common practice in organizations today. No longer can managers deny the power and practicality of praising. No longer can they fail to recognize a deserving employee because they couldn't think of something to do to show their appreciation. No longer will employees passively accept being ignored or be content to get feedback once a year, if then, during a performance review. No longer will using praise, recognition and rewards be optional in managing people."

Managers cannot use the excuse that they lack either the time or creativity to come up with ways to show appreciation to others. This is particularly true when we realize that the most powerful motivator is personalized, instant recognition. In a study conducted by Dr. Gerald H. Graham, professor of management at Wichita State University, it was determined that the top five motivating techniques for employees were:

- The manager personally congratulates employees who do a good job.

- The manager writes personal notes about good performance.

- The organization uses performance as the basis for promotion.

- The manager publicly recognizes employees for good performance.

- The manager holds morale-building meetings to celebrate successes.

For those who use cost as a reason not to reward or recognize employees, the most effective forms of recognition cost absolutely nothing. A pat on the back is a meaningful incentive. How much time and creativity does it take for a manager to pat someone on the back for a job well done?

According to Nelson (1994), in a survey conducted by the Minnesota Department of Natural Resources, it was determined that recognition activities contributed significantly to employee's job satisfaction. The survey data showed the following:

- 68 percent of the respondents said it was important to believe their work was appreciated by others

- 63 percent agreed that most people would like more recognition for their work

- 67 percent agreed that most people need appreciation for their work

- Only 8 percent thought that people should not look for praise for their work efforts

Good intentions that aren't acted upon mean nothing! All too often leaders ignore or underestimate the power of praise. In a time when competition is tough and retaining good employees is tougher, many leaders still don't effectively use praise as an incentive tool even though 76 percent of American workers ranked "recognition at a company meeting" as a meaningful incentive.

Native American cultures understood the value of appreciation. They knew giving an eagle feather was a way to symbolize the good work of others. The feather was proudly worn because it was not given lightly. Eagle feathers were given for the same reason the military gives medals and ribbons, to recognize the accomplishment of others. Perhaps the following true story will remind us about the importance of appreciation.

Just as Native Americans gave eagle feathers to show appreciation, we must symbolically give eagle feathers to all those deserving recognition. What we give to show recognition isn't nearly as important as the simple act of showing appreciation.

What should we recognize people for? We can start by recognizing acts of bravery, demonstrations of kindness, community service, a job well done, meeting or exceeding deadlines, or any of the attributes of wisdom.

To earn the Honored Feather of Wisdom for appreciation:

- Be attentive, actively search for people doing things right and recognize them.

- Overlook small failures.

- Recognize people publicly.

- Be honest in your recognition; don't recognize people when they don't deserve it.

- Find out what motivates people and use that to reward them.

- Recognition should follow the deserving act as quickly as possible.

- Reward those who recognize the accomplishment of others.

Reflective thoughts

Cheerfulness

"Those who know how to play can easily leap over the adversaries of life. And one who knows how to sing and laugh never brews mischief."

—Iglulik Eskimo Proverb

"One must laugh and greet each new day as a learning experience and as a special ceremony of life."

—Grandmother Louise Logan,
Cherokee

There is great wisdom in the Iglulik Eskimo proverb. The need to laugh is instinctive. Being around people who smile and laugh brings out the laughter in others. The ability and willingness to laugh is one of the most evident signs that we are dealing with someone who has a cheerful nature.

Cheerful people make life easier for themselves and everyone they come in contact with. Many organizations today include cheerfulness as one of the key attributes they look for when hiring. Who would hire a gloomy person over a person with a cheerful disposition? You can teach technological skills but you can't teach people to be cheerful. A cheerful disposition has great value.

Who are the cheerful people in your life? Isn't it amazing that the people who are most cheerful have the least to be cheerful about, while the ones who seem to carry a dark cloud overhead have a million reasons to be cheerful, but aren't. Cheerfulness is all about attitude. H. Stanley Judd had a great way of explaining attitude:

> "You may be dead broke and that's a reality, but in spirit you may be brimming over with optimism, joy, and energy. The reality of your life may result from many outside factors, none of which you can control. Your attitudes, however, reflect the ways in which you evaluate what is happening."

Cheerfulness can be related directly to a good sense of humor. Native American traditions had a common belief that humor was a necessary part of life. They believed that human beings were often weak and that their weaknesses led to doing foolish things. That is why clowns were important symbols in Native American cultures. Symbols reminded them of their weaknesses and the importance of smiling, laughter, and a sense of humor.

The attribute of cheerfulness brings us back to normality after dealing with such things as death, separation, sorrow, or all of the other traumatic events that bring stress into our lives. Cheerfulness eases the journey we take through life. Too much power and too much seriousness should be feared. Too much of a bad thing can create a great imbalance that impacts our community and us.

Indigenous people rightfully understood the importance of laughter and humor. It is only recently that we've again grasped this concept as critical to our physical health. Those who doubt the benefits of laughter and humor need only look to Norman Cousins. When he was told that he suffered from an incurable disease of the spine, he treated himself with reruns of comedy shows of Abbot and Costello, the Three Stooges, and Jack Benny. His book, *Anatomy of an Illness*, explained how he halted his illness through the use of laughter. Laughter actually alters the biochemistry by increasing peptide and endorphin levels in the bloodstream.

Norman Cousins might agree with Voltaire's comment, "In laughter, there is always a kind of joyousness that is incompatible with contempt or indignation…"

It is impossible to be sad or depressed when we're raucously laughing. Unfortunately, many of us have lost or reduced our capacity to laugh. Laughter is sometimes seen as silly or immature but actually; it is neither! Laughter is part of being human and is just as important for adults as it is for children. We need to laugh and play to thrive in body, mind, and spirit.

> "As adults, most of us have given up on playing. We're to busy, we believe-or we can't bring ourselves to behave in what we might consider frivolous ways. Most of us don't even think about playing anymore. Few people die, however, feeling that they did not work hard enough. When it is too late, the loss of play is what we too often regret. If we are already accustomed to playing, we must continue to upgrade our play, continue to find the time for it. If we don't play at all, then we must begin. In today's world, play is a lost key. It unlocks the door to our selves."
>
> —Lenore Terr, MD,
> *Beyond Love and Work*

In Native American mythology, the animal that best represents the concept of play is the coyote. Coyote is seen as a wild and wily teacher of the animal kingdom. Coyote is the old trickster who is known as the sacred clown. Coyote brings growth to everyone as well as the gift of trust. For play to exist we need trust. And for play to be readily accepted in business, particularly by skeptics, there must be the visible benefit of personal and organizational growth.

Native Americans understood the value of play due to their close observation of and relationship with animals. Terr (1999) explains that among the higher species, play does not stop with the assumption of adulthood.

"Play is biologically important to adult animals as well as to their young. In this regard, the everyday behavior of our own pets is interesting. Dogs don't stop their chasing and burrowing games just because they've grown up."

Diane Ackerman (1999), in her book *Deep Play*, emphasizes that animal play serves many purposes. That play is far older than humans. She explains that play can be a dress rehearsal for adult life, as when young mammals play courtship games, war games, socializing games, or motor-skill games. Ackerman explains:

"It's so familiar to us, so deeply ingrained in the matrix of our childhood, that we take it for granted...we may think of play as optional, a casual activity. But play is fundamental to evolution. Without play, humans and many other animals would perish."

Ackerman (1999) explains that animals may play in order to stay active and fit. Play allows primates to gather information about their environment. Horses that play keep in shape and are prepared for being chased by predators so they can react to danger properly. Play is often a way to establish social standing, ranking, and mate-finding.

For some persons, work is play. Yet many adults tend to lack a sense of playfulness in much of what they do. This is unfortunate since play is important for our health and happiness. We rarely see playfulness anywhere other than the local school playground. The enthusiasm and creativity of children can be enhanced by play. Likewise, the dullness of adults and society may well be associated with a lack of play.

Who cannot recall times in their youth when they were called home for dinner while in the middle of a neighborhood game? It was with reluctance that we left our friends and the game we were playing in order to eat dinner. Yet today, how often can we say we reluctantly leave anything when the opportunity for a meal exists? How many activities do we have in our adult lives that generate the same type of enthusiasm we felt as children while we were intensely distracted in playful activity? So what is play? Play is not just the absence of work, it is being actively engaged in something fun. The older we get, the less we tend to play. As adults we tend to work longer hours than ever before, sleep less, and reduce the number of hours we set aside for play. We've literally forgotten how to play; and few adults realize how important play is for personal development. Play can be linked to creativity, one of the most important qualities needed to be a valuable resource in today's workplace.

Somehow, our society has bought into the concept that work must be drudgery, while play is frivolous. We erroneously accepted the idea that play is something that only children are allowed to do.

Work and play do not have to be mutually exclusive. Many people find great pleasure in their work. Those who find the greatest pleasure in their work are the very best at what they do.

Swiss psychologist C. G. Jung understood that play and work should be inseparable. In 1923 he wrote, "Without playing with fantasy no creative work has ever yet come to birth." and, "The creation of something new is not accomplished by the intellect but by the play instinct acting from inner necessity. The creative mind plays with the objects it loves."

Terr (1999) agrees with Jung and provides insight into how play and work connect. According to Terr, play is defined as "activity directed primarily at having fun." She defines work as "activity directed primarily at personal and family sustenance, the achievement of power, the making of societal contributions; but work often carries with it a secondary goal-having fun." She goes on to explain:

> "We know we are playing when we are suddenly removed from all cares and worries. We know because afterward we feel cleansed and refreshed, despite our tired bodies, our aching muscles, our sleepiness. The interlude has been a healthy one. It takes place entirely outside, or at the very edge of, our drive for personal success or survival."

Play can be many different things to different people. It can be music, art, time spent on an enjoyable hobby, or special time with loved ones. Play might involve a camp out, fishing trip, hike through the woods, computer game, a good book or movie. Any activity where the true purpose is to have fun constitutes play. Play is lighthearted and enjoyable. It is not mean-spirited or conducted at the expense of others. Play brings pleasure and allows escape from the pressures of life.

Work and play should not be seen as opposites. There is a place for play at work. It may seem silly but more workplaces are encouraging an atmosphere of playfulness. This is particularly true in occupational settings where creativity is important to a business.

Toys for the boardroom and the office can now be found in various retail stores. Putty, foam balls and clay can be used to relieve stress or enhance creativity. Pencil sharpeners, cups, or clocks, designed in the images of cartoon characters adorn the desks and walls of many offices. Even screen savers can be used to add a sense of playfulness to ones work.

Playfulness seems to come less naturally as we get older. We therefore need to purposely set aside part of our time and energy for play. We need to assess our lives and determine whether we're spending enough time playing.

Incorporating work and play benefits both the individual and the organization. If you are not playing, now is a good time to start. Those who conduct professional research on play agree that the more a person plays, the easier it becomes to play, regardless of circumstances or age.

Cheryl Dahle (2000) gives an excellent example of how one company, aptly named "Play," turned play into a strategic advantage. This marketing boutique agency located in Richmond, Virginia, used the concept of play to run a very successful business. "Play" is made up of 31 people and delivers creative concepts, marketing and branding campaigns, promotional products, and event strategies. Its clients include American Express, Kalvin Klein, Nationwide Insurance, PricewaterhouseCoopers, Oscar Mayer, and Disney.

The corner office is actually called the "playroom." According to Dahle, the people at this company used play to generate over 70 ideas for the Weather Channel's marketing campaign. For most organizations, what the people at Play are doing would seem bizarre, but they are really working.

Dahle explains, "These folks aren't goofing off. They aren't fooling around. They're not even acting strangely. They're actually engaged in real work for an important client with a tight deadline."

The concept of play can be seen as a process to generate creative ideas, a movement that provides a competitive edge. Play at work appears to engender feelings of positive energy and closeness that are difficult to find in business settings. Refusing to pass judgment on others as they attempt to be creative enhances a creative self-fulfilling prophecy. It also brings genuine laughter and cheerfulness into the workplace.

> "Laughter and play on the job are not an end in and of themselves. They are a doorway, an entrée into being more human with the people we work with."
>
> —Matt Weinstein,
> *Managing to Have Fun*

The barriers to cheerfulness are many. Envy and jealousy are two of the challenges faced on an ongoing basis. Jamie Sams (1998) suggests the use of laughter as a defense against negative energies. She advises:

> "No harmful intent can flourish in the face of laughter. Laughter is the lubricant that keeps negativity from sticking. We break the stranglehold of any malicious intent when we do not fear it but rather engage in laughter, joy, and love. The more skillful we become, disengaging from negativity, the stronger we become spiritually, emotionally, mentally, and physically."

Using play and laughter as part of your management style makes perfect sense. This is particularly important for attracting and retaining talented individuals to work in organizations. For too many years, play and laughter were seen as an unnecessary evil to be avoided. After all, playing and laughing aren't productive.

In elementary school, learning and working with others was fun. It was okay as a child to learn through the playing of games. Then as the grade levels increased, play decreased. Eventually, play vanished and was replaced with work where we had to be serious all the time. "No time for play or games here, there is work to be done."

Native American games were derived from ancient ceremonies that dealt with healing, procreation, fertilization, birthing, and even catching-hunting. The games were built upon the concepts of four quarters, four seasons and the four elements. Over a period of time, the ceremonies gave way to games. Games survive as forms of amusement.

Rainbow Eagle (1996) explains that ceremony and ritual reflect passageways and building blocks for people to strengthen their relationships with the *Creator*. Ritual prevents holding onto anger or storing emotions that can turn into guilt or revenge. He states:

> "To Native people, ceremony was as common to daily life as it was to look to the sunrise or saying a prayer with the placing of tobacco or corn meal upon Mother Earth. From early childhood, Native children knew the nearness of the Great Mystery through their senses, dream time, their awareness of daily signs, by thinking of daily signs, stories, words of wisdom from their Elders, and their participation in and around ceremony."

The ball was the basic game tool and was originally considered to be a sacred object that was not touched by the hand. The ball was identified with spheres such as the sun and moon. Many of the games we now enjoy, such as soccer and basketball, have their origins from Native American games.

At the heart of Native American games was a form of spiritual training that is absent from the sports we participate in today. Native American games were known for instilling cooperation, competition and respect. There was a willingness to learn by listening to one's elders, by observing others and by practicing. The games that Native Americans played had to do with the spirit of play rather than the desire to win at all costs.

Have you ever noticed how adults seem to come alive at seminars when they are asked to play games? When we go to seminars, we expect to learn something new. The most popular seminars are the ones that teach while involving some type of physical or mental gaming activity.

Games can help us learn if they are designed properly. Games can teach us to survive, to more effectively dialogue, to understand others, and to sharpen mental or physical skills.

I recently went to my son, Sage's, grade school musical event. My wife and I were there to enjoy the lessons he had learned through the school's music program. I watched many parents file in with gloomy expressions on their faces and could tell that most of them were there because they felt obligated to attend the event.

The third graders sang songs and danced for their parents. The teachers and the kids were having a great time and I noticed that the parents were beginning to enjoy it too. Serious expressions turned to smiles as the children tried their best to entertain.

Before the program, Sage told us there was a secret about the school event we'd discover after we got there. We soon found out that the parents were to join their children for a special dance and that participation wasn't optional.

The parents came down from the bleachers and joined hands with their children. As the music began, we all moved in a circle around the room. Before long we were weaving in and out between other moms and dads who were holding hands with their own third graders. The smiles and laughter was every bit as discernable as the music that poured from the speakers that lined the gymnasium. By the end of the song everyone was smiling and laughing.

The gloomy faces that entered the gymnasium less than an hour before were now replaced with grins that spread from ear to ear. The energy level in the gymnasium was off the charts; what a remarkable change in such a short period of time. And why was that? They had taken a few minutes to play and laugh with others.

I wondered how long it had been since any of these adults had actually played and laughed? Did they have jobs that frowned on the idea of playfulness in the workplace? Did they realize the difference in their own countenances from the time they entered the gymnasium to when they finished dancing with their children?

As managers we often overlook the power of play and laughter at our own expense. If the last time you seriously played was at the playground when you were in elementary school, you may want to rethink the usefulness of play. I know I have. That is why some of my neighbors probably took a second look when Sage and I were busy making angels in the snow this winter. And the amazing thing is, it wasn't nearly as cold as I thought even though I was flat on my back in a foot of snow, flapping my arms and legs. Best of all, the imprint I made really looked like an angel.

Native American cultures share with us the importance of cheerfulness as an attribute of wisdom. We would be wise to learn from Native American cultures just how important it is to play and laugh. This is particularly important for adults who have lost this precious ability.

Native American cultures embraced play and laughter. We should do the same. Our ability to play and laugh is directly related to our ability to establish relationships and be more creative. Now, more than ever, the lessons of play and laughter that lead to cheerfulness are needed for our own personal development and the survival of our organizations.

To earn the Honored Feather of Wisdom for cheerfulness:

- Think back to your own childhood and the carefree times you spent playing and laughing. Try to relive those experiences.

- Spend time watching old comedy classics; the Three Stooges or Abbot and Costello are good for starters. If that is too slapstick for your tastes, watch something a little more sophisticated.

- Actively look for the humorous things that occur everyday and laugh at the silly things you see. It will become easier to do over time.

- Do something fun for a change. Be adventurous, go to a water park or a amusement park. Share in the children's laughter and excitement.

- Surround yourself with pictures and mementos that make you feel good. Create a personalized screensaver on your computer that makes you smile or laugh.

- If you liked playing sports as a kid, but you're not playing any type of sport now, join a team or league.

- If you don't play any type of musical instrument, now would be a good time to start.

- Spend time on a hobby that interests you.

Reflective thoughts

Dialogue

"You must speak straight so that your words may go as sunlight into our hearts."

—Cochise, Apache

"Dialogue is both rooted deeply in our ancestral past—helping us remember the sacredness and value of relationship-as well as being aligned with twenty-first century thinking, it can be seen as the bridge between where we are now and where we want to go."

—Linda Ellinor & Glenna Gerard,
Dialogue

"The most important work in the new economy is creating conversations."

—Alan Webber,
editor, *Fast Company* magazine

The ancient meaning of dialogue is *flow of meaning*. Dialogue is a key ingredient for effective communication. The modern passion for speed in all things has taken away from the art of really being able to dialogue with each other. We're in such a hurry to go from one meeting to another that quite often we fail to grasp why we're meeting.

A quote from David Bohm in his book *On Dialogue* may best explain the concept of dialogue:

> "From time to time, the tribe gathered in a circle. They just talked and talked and talked, apparently to no purpose. They made no decisions. There was no leader. And everybody could participate. There may have been wise men or wise women who were listened to a bit more-the older ones-but everybody could talk. The meeting went on, until it finally seemed to stop for no reason at all and the group dispersed. Yet after that, everybody seemed to know what to do, because they understood each other so well. Then they could get together in smaller groups and do something to decide things."

Dialogue is at the heart of great communications. But very often we do not enter into dialogue. Instead, we debate (beat down), or we discuss (break things up). And why is it we do not spend more time in real dialogue with others?

One reason is that dialoguing takes time. If you want to know if you're really communicating, just ask the people you meet with. Even kids will tell you whether you are spending time in dialogue versus debate or discussion. They won't use words like dialogue but you'll get the point. We can ask our families, friends or co-workers how we're doing in the dialogue department but we might not like their answer. The truth can be hard to handle sometimes.

Those who enter into dialogue are more likely to get the results they want. They are more likely to understand whom they are dealing with. They are also more likely to trust the people they are dialoguing with because they have at some level made an emotional connection.

The concept of dialogue is hard to put into a neat little package of key action steps. It is like so many other things we do; we know it is right just because it feels right.

Dialogue is experienced when we spend focused time with someone and express our true feelings without creating needless barriers. In fact, there is a simple way to break down communications barriers. Using this very effective piece of equipment increases the likelihood of dialogue, more effective meetings, and healthier relationships.

The object is called a "hot tub." It somehow loosens the tongue and opens the ears. It's a miracle device that guarantees close proximity to others and creates an air of informality. Dialogue may have been one of the ancillary benefits of the "sweat lodge."

Michael Kaplan (1998) wrote about this aspect of communications that finds relevance in a very odd setting. This historically Swedish custom has relevance to today's business environment. Kaplan explains how Nils Yngve Bergqvist, a hotelier in the northern Swedish village of Jukkasjarvi, helped launch the Sauna Academy.

The academy was founded to promote the greater good of sauna. Some would say the real advantage is to give the locals a cozy retreat for drinking beer and conversing on subjects of interest. The real importance of sauna as a Swedish tradition is dialogue. According to Kaplan:

> "Passing around a bottle of 160-proof Stroh 80, the doctor insists cleanliness and warmth were the initial attractions of the 500-year-old heat-bath tradition. 'It's how the [badly outnumbered] Finnish army beat up the Russians in many battles during World War II...It was a good way for the generals to meet with their men-you get undressed and everybody is equal. It's the same thing now.'
>
> 'With the sweat comes instant kinship and the same conversational intimacy fostered by poker tables and fishing holes.'...In the sauna you speak truth."

The *flow of water* may be closely aligned to the *flow of meaning*. Maybe the Romans were on to something with their concept of public baths. *If our meetings were more like informal gatherings, perhaps the flow of meaningful dialogue would become a natural process.*

We can trace the tradition of dialogue to the talking circles of Native Americans, the marketplaces of ancient Greece, and to the tribal customs of people from around the world. The practice of dialogue is as old as humanity itself. Unfortunately, the industrial age did a pretty good job of nearly erasing the practice of dialogue from the world. The voices of the human cogs in the wheel of commerce didn't need to be heard, or so it was believed. Yet we are seeing a re-emergence of dialogue throughout our organizations.

This re-emergence can energize an organization and bring about new levels of collaboration that haven't been seen since our ancestors spoke around the tribal campfires. Dialogue should be seen as an extremely important tool that can be used to foster more effective teamwork and a greater sense of community within our organizations.

Linda Ellinor and Glenna Gerard, cofounders of the *Dialogue Group*, wrote the following concerning dialogue:

> "It is both rooted deeply in our ancestral past-helping us remember the sacredness and value of relationship-as well as being aligned with twenty-first century thinking, it can be seen as the bridge between where we are now and where we want to go."

They explain that dialogue is a practice that actually bridges communication, leadership, and culture. A critical factor in this practice is the concept of trust. For without trust, true dialogue is impossible.

Trust is the cornerstone for building relationships with others. Without solid relationships, people will not bridge the gap between communication and true dialogue.

Building trust requires taking the time to deeply listen to what others have to say. As important as effective listening is, it is difficult to find training that focus on this concept. Listening is sometimes treated as a relatively unimportant area of personal self-development. Many understand the importance of dialogue on an intellectual level but few actually practice it.

There is a simple rule that greatly enhances our ability to enter into dialogue: spend 80 percent of our time genuinely listening with compassion and only 20 percent talking. It's not a perfect rule but it is better than when the percentages are reversed.

> "Dialogue is not just talking with one another. More than speaking, it is a special way of listening to one another-listening without resistance...it is listening from a stand of being willing to be influenced."
>
> —Anonymous

> "People do not listen, they reload."
>
> —Anonymous

We often prepare ourselves before we speak. What seems to be lacking is the same amount of preparation when we listen. One way to prepare to listen is to be still and quiet the inner voice as our tribal ancestors did. They were attuned to their surroundings; their language was deeply rooted in the physical sounds of the earth, the birds and the beasts, the flow of streams and rivers. We need to ask ourselves, what is our language deeply rooted to?

To really listen, first be still and look for the meaning in the words of others. Observe their reactions and the responses you have to their words. It is only after listening that you can effectively speak.

We admire those who speak their mind and their heart. Yet, how can we do this if we haven't taken the time to listen? Isaacs (1999) states:

> "If I speak, it is often to make my point, to indicate my superiority to claim my ground. Often I lie in wait in meetings, like a hunter looking for his prey, ready to spring out at the first moment of silence. My gun is loaded with pre-established thoughts. I take aim and fire, the context irrelevant, my bullet and its release all that matter to me."

Studies show that women and men communicate differently. Our culture can be unkind to those who cross the invisible border that separates gender-based communication. Conversational rituals exist and differ based upon gender. According to Dr. Tannen (1994), men use opposition such as banter, joking, teasing, playful put-downs, and expend effort to avoid the one-down position in interaction.

Conversational rituals common among women are often ways of maintaining an appearance of equality. Women take into account the effect of the exchange on the other person. They expend effort to downplay the speaker's authority so they can get the job done without flexing their muscles in an obvious way.

Dr. Tannen (1994) goes on to say:

> "Men whose oppositional strategies are interpreted literally may be seen as hostile when they are not, and their efforts to ensure that they avoid appearing one-down may be taken as arrogance. When women use conversational strategies designed to avoid appearing boastful and to take the other person's feelings into account, they may be seen as less confident and competent than they really are."

Good leaders understand the differences in gender-based communication styles. Men downplay their doubts while women downplay their certainty. Understanding these different styles are critical in making well-informed decisions. Just because people seem absolutely sure of something doesn't mean they really have a clue as to what is going on. On the other hand, just because others appear to be unconfident doesn't mean they don't understand what is going on.

Anthropologist Marjorie Harness Goodwin found that young girls criticize other girls who displayed self-confidence. Sounding too sure of themselves made these girls unpopular with their peers. Therefore, social inhibitions against boastful appearances can make women appear less confident than they really are.

Goodwin found that young girls discover they get better results if they phrase their ideas as suggestions rather than orders. Giving reasons for their suggestions in terms of the good of the group also helped. But while these ways of talking make girls and, later, women-more likable, they make them seem less competent and self-assured in the world of work.

There are no hard and fast rules that apply to everyone, regardless of gender. Unfortunately, some people have overly high expectations about how men and women should communicate. In their minds, men who are not very aggressive or women who are too aggressive just don't compute. The difference between being seen as a go-getter or as being arrogant is a matter of degree, and the formula is different for each individual. Being aware of this dynamic allows us to relate more effectively with others.

In William Isaacs', *Dialogue and the Art of Thinking* (1999), Peter Senge wrote that after a speech to a large group in Silicon Valley, he was asked to meet with twenty-five executives, mostly CEOs and executive VPs. Rather than speak more or have a question and answer session, he suggested that the group put their chairs in a circle and do a "check-in." This simple practice of dialogue involved each person saying a few words about their thoughts and feelings at the time.

Many cultures have nurtured dialogue by sitting in a circle and talking. Council circles, women's circles and circles of elders have been used universally to enter into dialogue. This form of meeting allows for a shared inquiry that is reflective in nature. Today, we have replaced the council fire with the boardroom and we have lost something in the process. In tribal gatherings, community events, and councils, conversations often took place around a fire and lasted for days. The conversation typically included everyone in a tribe. Men, women and children were included in conversations and were all treated with respect.

Considerable power can be unleashed in dialogue. Today we often fall back on argument and debate as a form of communication when the going gets tough. In business, our language stems more from the "machine age" than from our ancient memories of dialogue. Fortunately, ancient memories of dialogue still burn in us much like the tribal fires that burned brightly long ago. These embers can be re-ignited to tap the power of dialogue.

Isaacs (1999) cites recent studies of the survival habits of emperor penguins in Antarctica. It had been a mystery how these animals could survive intense winds and frigid temperatures of this strange continent. Temperatures of fifty degrees below zero Fahrenheit and winds of one hundred miles an hour or more are not uncommon there. They survive by forming circles, with their bodies nestled together, to retain heat. They slowly rotate the circle so that no one bird is exposed to the wind too long.

Forming a circle is an apt metaphor for the power of dialogue in dealing with the challenges of life. *Forming a circle and using dialogue effectively can help us survive.*

This lesson was desperately needed when the 104th Congress literally shut down the federal government over the budget battles with President Clinton. By late 1996, David Skaggs, a five-term Democratic congressman, had seen and heard enough of the hostile conflict among his fellow legislators. He decided to do something about this poisonous political process.

In March of 1997, 215 members of the House attended a three-day retreat in Hersey, Pennsylvania, without the media or their staff members. Their spouses participated in the meetings, and their children also attended. One of the most successful parts of the retreat was a train ride that allowed the legislators to see each other with their families in a non-adversarial role. The conversational tone that developed during the retreat would become known as the "Spirit of Hershey."

Have you ever closely observed the rituals that take place in a business meeting? If so, you've noticed "ego muscles" being flexed, more talking than listening going on, and a tendency to protect ones turf at all costs. Meetings don't have to be run this way but that is often what happens.

In Native American council meetings, a talking stick was passed to signify who had the floor. This ritual prevented cross talk from occurring, honored the words, and showed respect for the person holding it.

The talking stick came to us from indigenous peoples who used it to call for respectful listening. Here's how it works. The person who holds the stick speaks to the group and shares whatever wisdom they have to offer. Each speaker, in turn, picks up the stick, speaks, and then either places the stick in the center of the circle or passes it to the next speaker.

Having nothing to say is okay. You are not obligated to speak. Sometimes, the real value we receive in meeting with others is to just listen. We really need to hear what is being said and absorb the words of others for future reference.

We can become so accustomed to the places we normally meet and the people we normally meet with, that the idea of a better way of meeting doesn't even cross our minds. Anyone who has used "Robert's Rules of Order" knows, there has to be a better way to meet.

A better way of meeting is a non-traditional style. In this meeting we sit at tables in a circle and everyone has the opportunity to share their thoughts on the subject matter presented by co-leaders. This form of communicating and listening can be described as transformational conversation. Through this type of meeting, people tap into a higher level of self and group awareness. A shift in their thinking, actions, and relationships with others is created.

This form of meeting is similar to how the ancients met around council fires. This approach was lost to us and is now reappearing in our boardrooms and centers of higher learning. Installing fire circles in our meeting areas might not be possible, however; we can alter our traditional decision making models and ascend to a new meeting mode that suspends judgment until everyone has had an opportunity to express themselves.

Jamie Sams (1998) explains that in the tradition of the Southern Seers, one can speak from a voice that is called "the clear lake." We can speak, feel, and think like a clear lake by simply allowing all of our thoughts, feelings, and the words of others to be heard, to be felt, and to pass through us with ease. Sams goes on to say, "We also have the ability to interact without reacting, viewing any situation as an unbiased observer who can see the obvious, feel all of the emotions with ease, keep the mind clear of chatter, and still maintain a neutral point of view."

We should think of our meeting space as a modern day kiva. The kiva is a sacred ceremonial chamber that is still used by the Pueblo people for religious functions. It is expressive of the four elements and embodies the characteristics of each. The kiva resides under ground and is representative of Mother Earth. Within the kiva you will find round walls and a constantly lit fire that draws life from the air that surrounds it. A water jar symbolizes the element of water. The primordial components of life, earth, air, fire, and water are all included in the kiva.

Fire is the first element and it represents power, procreation and destruction. Water is liquid and therefore represents blood, sweat, tears, urine and sperm. Water can also be destructive; therefore its ways must be known and understood. Earth is the fruitful source of all life. Earth represents bounty, femininity, harmony, and order.

Indigenous people understood the sacredness of dialogue. They understood that their words had power, the power to shape future events and the power to affect others. Today we are mostly concerned with finding open space in order to conduct business. The concept of a kiva adds sacredness to the dialogue that takes place when human beings come together to interact.

To earn the Honored Feather of Wisdom for dialogue:

- Put people at ease. Take time to meet and greet all those present. Do this with a smile and a well-intentioned handshake.

- Make eye contact with those in your group and use their names when speaking to them or when clarifying statements they have made.

- Don't assume a position of authority but let those in your group know you are part of the group and that everyone's input is of equal value.

- Use good meeting management techniques. Let people know why you are meeting, and ensure they have input as to the objectives of the meeting.

- Be aware that some people are uncomfortable in groups. If they are not openly contributing to the dialogue, draw them out by asking their opinion.

- Be present throughout the dialogue and listen much more than you speak.

- Suspend your desire to come up with a decision as soon as someone expresses a concern.

- Never forget the sacredness that exists when people are gathered together in dialogue.

Reflective thoughts

Honesty

"It does not require many words to speak the truth."

—Chief Joseph

"Treachery darkens the chain of friendship, but truth makes it brighter than ever."

—Conestoga proverb

One of the preeminent figures in Native American history was Sitting Bull of the Hunkpapa division of the Sioux tribe. This man, who exemplified the Plains spirit of the nineteenth century, was born in 1834 and was called Jumping Badger as a boy. He accompanied his father into battle at the age of 14. In 1848, his name became Tatanka Yotaka, which literally means "sitting buffalo bull" but he was simply known as Sitting Bull after he became a shaman in 1857.

Sitting Bull quickly acquired influence among his people because, in part, he was known for his blunt honesty and ability as a peacemaker. He was known for his eloquence and steadfastness in speaking out for the rights of his people. He expected those who agreed to a treaty to live up to their promises.

Major James McLaughlin wrote of Sitting Bull, "His accuracy of judgment, knowledge of men, a student-like disposition to observe natural phenomena, and a deep insight into affairs among Indians and such white people as he came into contact with, made his stock in trade, and made good medicine."

He was admired by his people and was respected for his generosity, quiet disposition, and his steadfast adherence to the ideals espoused by Native American culture. Among those ideals, he was certainly known for the way he honestly dealt with others.

Part of his address in 1883 to the Government Peace Commission stresses the importance he placed on honesty:

> "Now I will tell you my mind and I will tell everything straight. I know the Great Spirit is looking down upon me from above and will hear what I say. Therefore I will do my best to talk straight, and I hope that someone will listen to my wishes and help me to carry them out."

Thomas Jefferson said, "Honesty is the first chapter of the book of wisdom." *Honesty is one of the most important attributes of wisdom.* I shared the importance of this attribute with my son recently.

We were in the back yard as our Old English Sheepdog (Poppy) ran circles around the spot where we stood. I noticed Sage running towards the back door without saying anything. I knew immediately something was wrong.

I went into to house to check on him and could tell immediately from his tear streaked face that he had been crying. He didn't want to tell me what was wrong but I insisted. He finally admitted tearfully that a neighborhood boy had punched him in the stomach.

I was furious. Sage was only seven years old, a very gentle child, and the boy who hit him was twice his size and several years older. Having been roughed up by bullies myself as a child; I was horrified that he had been physically attacked when his major concern should be who to play with rather than undergoing the trauma of a physical attack.

As I headed toward the door to go to the boy's house to speak to his parents, Sage shifted from tears that expressed the hurt of being attacked to something that could better be defined as wailing. He tried to keep me from confronting the boy and his parents. I passed this off as fear of embarrassment or retaliation, but I knew through experience that hurtful situations, unlike wine, do not improve with time.

After I stormed to the house where Sage had been hurt, I asked the boy to get his parents. I wasn't going to tolerate this type of behavior, particularly when it affected a child.

I was surprised to find out that Sage had not been hit. According to the kids playing there, he had been teased and in his anger he had called the bigger boy a bad word. I explained to the kids that teasing was no way to treat others and that bad language was inappropriate as well.

Needless to say, I went home with a different view of events than the one I left the house with. After explaining to Sage that I wanted to know what really happened, he broke down in tears. He explained that the older boy was teasing him and the bad word just came out. The tears he shed were tears of shame for using language he knew he was not allowed to use. He decided to say the boy hit him rather than admit to calling him a bad name.

I was angry with Sage for using unacceptable language but I was relieved that he knew his behavior and the behavior of the bigger boy were wrong. We explained to Sage that what really upset us was that he lied about what happened. We understood what it was like to be angry when someone picks on you and to say something you regret later. What we did not accept was being dishonest about what had really happened.

There is always going to be someone bigger than you are. Others might tower over you physically or have positional power over you within your organization. How we deal with these people says a lot about what we hold to be self-truths. As George Bernard Shaw once said: "We must make the world honest before we can honestly say to our children that honesty is the best policy."

My hope is that Sage learned that dishonesty is not an option. That in all his dealings with other children and with adults, no matter how painful, being honest is the only option. No matter what the circumstances, he can always be honest with me. In fact, I expect it. After all, it is one of the most important attributes of wisdom. We named him "Sage" for a reason.

There is a Native American Cinderella story where honesty is rewarded and dishonesty punished. Cyrus Macmillan recorded the story in Canada in the early part of the twentieth century. According to North American mythology, there was a god of the Eastern woodlands named Strong Wind.

Strong Wind was a great Indian warrior who could make himself invisible. He lived with his sister on the Atlantic coast. Because of his mighty deeds, many maidens sought him. It was widely known that he would marry the first maiden who could see him as he came home at night. To determine whether the maidens who wanted to marry him were honest, he made himself invisible and his sister asked the maidens whether they could see him. They would all say they could see him when asked, and so he refused to marry any of them.

There were three sisters who hoped to marry Strong Wind. The youngest of the three was very beautiful and gentle and well loved by all. Her older sisters were jealous and treated her cruelly. The sisters clothed her in rags that she might be ugly; they cut off her long black hair; and they burned her face with coals from the fire that she might be scarred and disfigured. But the young girl was patient and kept her gentle heart and went gladly about her work.

When the older sisters were asked if they could see Strong Wind they were also untruthful. The younger sister decided that she would also seek to marry Strong Wind. She was asked if she could see him but she honestly said she couldn't. Because she told the truth, he made himself visible to her. Strong Wind's sister took her home and bathed her: all of her scars disappeared from her face and body, and her hair grew long and black again like the raven's wing. She was given fine clothes and rich ornaments to wear.

Strong Wind took her to be his bride. The girl's two elder sisters were very cross and they wondered at what had happened. Strong Wind knew of their cruelty and resolved to punish them. He used his great power and changed them both into aspen trees and rooted them in the earth. And ever since that day, the leaves of the aspen have always trembled, and they shiver in fear at the approach of Strong Wind. It makes no difference how softly the wind comes, for they are still mindful of his great power and anger because of their dishonesty and cruelty to their sister so long ago.

Just like Sitting Bull, we must live authentic and honest lives. *Honesty is an attribute of wisdom that is required for any lasting and meaningful relationship with others.* The lack of trust in government, politics, the media, and business are directly related to our perception of dishonest behavior.

In *USA Today*, it was reported that forty percent of workers from a variety of industries in companies with 100 or more employees knew of ethical or legal violations at their company in the past two years. Sixteen percent of those surveyed knew about lying on reports and records. Fifteen percent of those surveyed were aware of employees lying to their supervisors.

It might even be worse than that. According to Alice Van Housen in her article, *Here's a Radical Idea—Tell the Truth*, in a recent survey of 40,000 Americans, 93% admitted to lying "regularly and habitually in the workplace." She goes on to say that lying causes stress, anxiety, and depression.

William J. Bennett (1993) may have best expressed the price we pay for dishonesty and the reward we reap for honesty.

> "To be dishonest is to be partly feigned, forged, fake, or fictitious. Honesty expresses both self-respect and respect for others. Dishonesty fully respects neither oneself nor others. Honesty imbues lives with openness, reliability, and candor; it expresses a disposition to live in the light. Dishonesty seeks shade, cover, or concealment. It is a disposition to live partly in the dark."

In modern society, stretching the truth to the breaking point is often considered an acceptable practice. In some professions, winning is more important than justice, even when the truth is horribly distorted or conveniently misplaced.

In Native American cultures you couldn't be respected as a person or elevated to a position of honor unless you were known to be honest. A common attribute of great leaders is honesty. That is why Sitting Bull was a Chief. He was brave enough to be honest with his people and with his enemies. Today, we can learn much from him.

To earn the Honored Feather of Wisdom for honesty:

- Share your true thoughts and feelings with others.

- If you must express something that might be hurtful to others, do so in a caring way.

- Always remember to look for the good in others.

- Weigh your words carefully, once you have spoken, your words cannot be taken back.

- Don't expect that everyone will like what you have to say.

- Keep your promises.

Reflective thoughts

Humility

"But for the rest of us, a soft, low voice has always been considered an excellent thing, in a man as well as in a woman. Even the warrior who inspired the greatest terror in the hearts of his enemies was, as a rule, a man of the most exemplary gentleness, and almost feminine refinement, among his family and friends. And though we are capable of strong and durable feelings, we are not demonstrative in our affection at any time, especially in the presence of guests or strangers."

—Ohiyesa

A Santee Sioux, Charles Alexander Eastman (Ohiyesa), said the first Americans mingled their pride with humility. This was shown through a profound belief in silence. Silence was seen as the absolute poise or balance of the body, mind and spirit.

Chief Luther Standing Bear, a Teton Sioux, said that silence was meaningful with the Lakota. A space of silence was needed before talking. To be polite, it always helped to think before speaking since the alternative could be disastrous. He also said:

> "And in the midst of sorrow, sickness, death, or misfortune of any kind, and in the presence of the notable and great, silence was the mark of respect. More powerful than words was silence with the Lakota."

Native American orators were very proficient at arranging their thoughts because of the deep contemplation they observed in their youth. By listening to the warbling of birds and by observing the beauties of the forest, and all of the marvelous aspects of nature, they were furnished with an abundance of reflective opportunities. Chief Oren Lyons can see the reflective nature of Native American orators in the following poem in his address to the Non-Governmental Organizations of the United Nations in Geneva, Switzerland.

Consciousness

I do not see a delegation
For the Four-footed.
I see no seat for the eagles.

We forget and we consider
Ourselves superior.
But we are after all
A mere part of the Creation.

And we must consider
To understand where we are.

And we stand somewhere between
The mountain and the Ant.

Somewhere and only there
As part and parcel
Of the Creation.

In *All Roads are Good*, Abe Conklin is cited as a dancer, storyteller and leader among the Poncas. He states that "the only perfect person is Wakonda, so when the Poncas made something, they would put in an odd bead or in some way break the pattern so it wouldn't be perfect. This was to keep us humble-only God can make something perfectly."

In most native cultures, the people who are leaders are often the most humble. Humility among native people is a quiet acceptance of who a person is. Quiet acceptance of ones skills and talents is valued over boastfulness and arrogance.

As Americans, we tend to value those hero-leaders who have proven they accomplish great feats single-handedly. They are the miracle workers who are totally independent and have no need of others to meet difficult mission requirements. But it is rare that anyone can achieve anything of significance without the help of others. There are always those in the background who have worked and sacrificed to meet the needs of every worthwhile endeavor.

Leaders who show true humility give credit to all the people who have participated in successes while addressing their own weaknesses in order to improve personal performance. They respect the work and effort of those who have given unselfishly of themselves. Personal gratification is postponed in order to reward the real heroes of the organization.

Murphy and Snell (1994) call this concept strategic humility. They point out that, over time, great leaders have understood the value of strategic humility. Lincoln, Churchill, and even Sam Walton launched their journeys of leadership by recognizing and addressing their own weaknesses. They learned from their mistakes and were not immobilized because they made the wrong decision from time to time. They learned and then they moved on.

In Native American cultures it was *bear* who most embodied the attribute of humility which is nurtured during quiet self-observation. Every winter, bear retires to its cave to reflect upon the events of the past year. It finds the answers to its questions in the silence and emptiness of its cave.

Silence and solitude help us find ourselves. This is no simple task when we are part of a very busy world. People and issues tug at us all the time. It isn't easy finding the time or the place for silence and self-reflection. Occasionally, we must take the time to step back from the noisy world in order to hear the voice of our higher self. It is through a personal canon that embraces self-reflection that leaders grasp the really significant issues. It is in understanding ourselves that self-confidence is gained. Self-confidence leads to the attribute of humility.

To earn the Honored Feather of Wisdom for humility:

- Bear can go to his cave. Set aside a location for quiet contemplation.

- Set aside time for reflective thinking.

- During exercise, put your thoughts and concerns in order.

- Take yourself to lunch and spend that time in reflective thought.

- Set aside a special time and place every day for journaling. You'll be surprised at how easily the words will flow when you are in reflective mood.

Reflective thoughts

Loyalty

"There is no more disgraceful page in the history of our relations with the American Indians than that which conceals the treachery visited upon the Chiricahuas who remained faithful in their allegiance to our people."

—John G. Bourke

Being loyal means being true to your beliefs. It means being there when you are needed. As children, we learn about loyalty from our families. Even at an early age, we receive recognition as being faithful and someone whom can be confided in. A loyal person keeps the best interest of others at heart no matter what; it is the right thing to do.

Colin Greer and Herbert Kohl (1995) in *A Call to Character*, explain loyalty as follows:

> "People will recognize you as faithful if they can safely confide in you, if you honor them even in their absence, and if you protect their best interests when it is in your power to do so. Do not forget the people and ideas you've been close to. There is great comfort for those who know you, if they can be sure of you even during long periods of separation."

Dogs are exemplary teachers of loyalty. Everyday when I get home, Poppy, our Old English Sheepdog is waiting at the top of the stairs. Our daily routine of greeting each other is something I look forward to.

I've always had a fondness for Old English Sheepdogs. I'm not sure why, maybe it was all those Disney or Doris Day movies I grew up with. Regardless, three years ago when we decided to get a dog, I knew I wanted that breed.

We picked her out of a litter that appeared to be rapidly moving balls of hair. We were somehow fooled into thinking she was the most laid-back pup in the litter. We did potty training, and puppy kindergarten. Before classes were over, Poppy actually learned to ring a bell whenever she needed to go outside (this still amazes me). Until recently I really believe she thought our son Sage, was also a puppy. At least that was my impression whenever I would see them rolling around on the floor together. Poppy has, in every sense of the word, become a loyal and integral part of our family.

Dogs have been considered the embodiment of loyalty for eons. They protect our homes and our families. They give unconditional love even when we don't deserve it. Their sense of service to their owners is unparalleled in the animal kingdom. That is why those who are considered in the Native American culture to have dog medicine, are the people who embody the concept of service to others.

Jamie Sams and David Carson explain that the message dogs are trying to give us is that we must delve deeply into our sense of service to others.

> "Canines are genuinely service-oriented animals, and are devoted to their owners with a sense of loyalty that supersedes how they are treated...If dog has

been yelled at or paddled, it still returns love to the person who was the source of its bad treatment. This does not come from stupidity, but rather from a deep and compassionate understanding of human shortcomings. It is as if a tolerant spirit dwells in the heart of every canine that asks only to be of service."

For those of us with less than four legs, being loyal means being there when we are needed. Our loyalties are important signs of the kinds of persons we have chosen to become. Loyal people are steadfast in their attachments to the people they associate with. They seriously care for the well being of others. William J. Bennett (1993) explains:

"Ceremonial expressions aside, loyalty is like courage in that it shows itself most clearly when we are operating under stress. Real loyalty endures inconvenience, withstands temptation, and does not cringe under assault. Yet the trust that genuine loyalty tends to generate can pervade our whole lives."

Tony Schwartz (2000) knows that companies are looking for ways to make themselves more alluring to employees. He found that the single most important variable in employee productivity and loyalty turns out to be neither pay, perks or environment. Rather, according to the *Gallup Organization*:

"It's the quality of the relationship between employees and their direct supervisors. More specifically, what people want most from their supervisors is the same things that kids want most from their parents: someone who sets clear and consistent expectations, cares for them, values their unique qualities, and encourages and supports their growth and development. Put another way, the greatest sources of satisfaction in the workplace are internal and emotional."

What can be more internal or emotional than loyalty? The Kickapoo, a midwestern tribe that was noted for its frequent wanderings, tell a story of great loyalty. The Kickapoo still honor two brave women who are remembered in song and dance because of their great courage and noble sacrifice made for their tribe. This is the story that the people heard:

A band of men and women of the Kickapoo were hunting in a distant territory when they were attacked by a war party from another tribe. The Kickapoo who were not killed or badly wounded escaped down into some gorges and hid in a great cave beneath the thundering falls of a mighty river. All the members of the band knew about the hiding place.

Two of the women from the Kickapoo band were taken back to the enemy camp as prisoners. For many days the enemy warriors searched for the Kickapoo survivors without any success.

After having a dream, the medicine man of the enemy tribe told his chief that the two prisoners knew where to find the remaining Kickapoo. After calling a council of war, the chief had the prisoners brought to him. The women were tortured with blazing twigs that were held to their wrists. They eventually agreed to reveal the hiding place of their band. For a moment, they spoke softly together in their own dialect and then, by signs, showed that they were ready to lead them.

The two women pointed to the river instead of leading the way into the forest. By signs, they showed that their people were far away and could be reached quicker by the warriors if they went by canoe. When the chief pointed toward the forest and his braves pushed the women in that direction, they showed by sign talk that they could not lead the warriors by land. Only by water did they know the way to the hidden Kickapoo band.

After paddling far, the chief asked the women if they were not yet near the hiding place of his enemies. The women sign-talked that the place was near. From the distance came the thunder of the falls. The chief was brave, but even he feared the mighty force of the swift-rushing waters. He was directly behind the two captive women who sat in the bow. He touched them on the shoulders, and they turned to him at once. The chief ceased to fear when he saw that both women were smiling.

Too late, the chief and warriors knew that they had been tricked. The bravest had but time to sing a few notes of their death songs before the raging torrent swept the shattered canoes over the crest of the waterfall. Proudly leading the band of enemy warriors to death on the jagged rocks below were the two brave women of the Kickapoo.

Loyalty is developed over time. It is tested when we take up for friends when they are being harassed and harangued by others. We show loyalty when faithful to others even when faced with collusion, ridicule and even violence. Loyalty is the embodiment of service.

To earn the Honored Feather of Wisdom for loyalty:

- Take time to determine what your core beliefs and values are, then stick to them.

- Always keep the interests of your friends and acquaintances at heart no matter what.

- Honor others, even when they are absent.

- Embrace a tolerant spirit with a deep compassion for the shortcomings of others.

Reflective thoughts

ATTRIBUTES OF THE GUIDE

Courage

"No person among us desires any other reward for performing a brave and worthy action, but the consciousness of having served his nation."

—Thayendanegea,
a Mohawk

What is courage? For some, it means literally sacrificing themselves for the benefit of others. For others, it means finding their voice and saying what needs to be said.

We expect our leaders to be courageous. We expect them to proudly carry our organizational banner and set an example we are proud to emulate. Great leaders are courageous. They respect the courageous acts of others and willingly recognize those who go above and beyond the call of duty.

We often attribute courage to the brave acts of warriors. Native Americans had a rich heritage of bravery and courageous service to their people. Well-known courageous Native American chiefs with acts of bravery included: Pontiac, Red Jacket, Tecumseh, Red Cloud, Sitting Bull, Joseph, Crazy Horse, and Geronimo. These names, however; only scratch the surface of those who showed great courage in defending the beliefs they held so dearly.

In Native American cultures, the bravest acts were not in taking the life of one's enemy, but rather, were abstaining from the taking of life. That is why Crazy Horse was so well known for his bravery and honor. When he pursued the enemy into their stronghold, he often refrained from killing and would simply strike them with a switch. This showed that he did not fear their weapons or even care to waste his time upon them.

Courage was not limited to acts of bravery that required the defeat of an enemy. A courageous act might have been inspired through the accomplishment of a good deed. An old chief when speaking to a scout who was seeking buffalo in midwinter for his starving people expressed this type of courage:

> "Let neither cold, hunger, nor pain, nor the fear of them, neither the bristling teeth of danger, nor the very jaws of death itself, prevent you from doing a good deed."

Much of the courage and bravery of Native Americans was captured in a report entitled *Native American Military Heroes*, written for the Defense Equal Opportunity Management Institute by Lieutenant Andrew H. Henderson. According to Henderson (1998):

> "Native Americans have fought in every American war. During the American Revolution the Oneida and Tuscarora sided with the American Revolutionaries. The Creeks and Cherokees aided the colonials while members of the Stockbridge Indian Tribe enlisted as minutemen in Massachusetts."

Native Americans fought on both sides of the Civil War. Ely S. Parker, a Seneca, served as military secretary to General Ulysses S. Grant. He later became the first Native American to become a Brigadier General in the United States Army. Native Americans also served during the Spanish American War and rode with the Rough Riders in the famous charge up San Juan Hill.

During World War I, nearly 12,000 Native Americans joined the United States Armed Forces. Army veteran Jed Joseph Johnson from Oklahoma, who served as a United States Congressman from 1927–1947, remarked:

> "I served with many full-blood Indians and part-Indians during World War I in France. I saw them in action in the front lines, and I was deeply impressed with their valor and courage. There were no better or braver soldiers than were the American Indians."

A Choctaw Indian demonstrated great courage in World War I. Private Joseph Oklahombi, from Company D of the 141st Infantry. With several other soldiers, Oklahombi crossed barbed wire into "No Man's Land" along the Franco-German border to take out German machine-gun nests. Under a violent rain of fire, Oklahombi crossed 200 yards of barbed wire entanglements and stormed a strongly held position containing more than 50 German machine-guns and a number of trench mortars. He then turned the weapon on the enemy and ultimately captured 171 German prisoners, single handedly. He also crossed the battlefield back and forth under a continuous barrage of fire, pinpointing enemy positions and rescuing wounded companions. For these acts of heroism and bravery, Oklahombi was awarded the prestigious *Croix de Gerre* by the French, and became one of the most decorated Native American veterans of the war.

During World War II, Native American participation in the Armed Forces swelled to nearly 25,000. These men and women received 71 Air Medals, 51 Silver Stars, 47 Bronze Stars, 34 Distinguished Flying Crosses, and 6 Medals of Honor. Native Americans were zealous to serve during World War II. According to Army officials, the draft would have been unnecessary if the country's entire population had enlisted in the same proportion, as did Native Americans.

One of the most famous heroes to emerge from World War II was PFC Ira Hamilton Hayes of the USMC. Hayes was a full-blooded Pima who joined the Marines in 1942 and saw action as a paratrooper throughout the Pacific. In February of 1945, he landed as part of the Fifth Marine Division assault on Iwo Jima and took part in a forward attack on Mount Suribachi. In the midst of heavy enemy fire, Hayes and five other Marines raised Old Glory on the volcanic peak of Mount Suribachi. An *Associated Press* photographer caught the image on film, creating one of the most inspiring-and recognized-war photographs ever taken. This awesome moment is captured in bronze at the war memorial in our nation's capitol for all to see.

It is estimated that between 10,000 and 15,000 Native Americans served in the Korean War while approximately 42,500 served in the Vietnam War and 3,000 served in the Gulf War. Regardless of the number, Native Americans have a reputation for being courageous warriors. Many Native Americans have received the highest honor our nation can give for bravery.

The United States Government understands the importance of courage and the value of those who show what courage is all about. Possibly the finest examples of proven courage in our nation are the recipients of the Medal of Honor. The recipients of this prestigious award are those who often gave their lives in order to protect others.

One of the most well known recipients of this award was Colonel Gregory "Pappy" Boyington, who served as commander of the famous "Black Sheep". Boyington, a part-Native American, was the ranking American "ace" of the era with 28 dogfight victories to his credit. Eventually, Boyington was shot down and captured by the Japanese. He survived 20 months of maltreatment and beatings at the hands of his captors.

Colonel Boyington and many other Native Americans earned the respect of their country through their numerous acts of courage. Many earned military honors just as their ancestors earned feathers for courageous acts that benefited their people.

Courage is often accompanied with a spirit of humility. The most courageous people you will ever meet are the ones who refuse to sing their own praises. Peter F. Drucker (1996) said "effective leaders are not preachers, they are doers."

Courage is not just an attribute that is exhibited within the military. Acts of courage are evident within all types of organizations; courageous acts are admirable wherever they transpire. Bravery is welcomed and needed in all types and sizes of businesses. Much like the fighting that takes place on the battlefield, some modern organizations are fighting for their survival.

Who is doing the fighting where you work? It takes courage to be on the front line. There is a certain amount of risk involved in doing the things that need to be done. Whether in the public, private, or nonprofit sector, it makes no difference: all need to be courageous to survive and thrive.

We all fear risk taking to a certain degree. Fear keeps some of our most talented people from sharing creative ideas. Ideas are the lifeblood of our organizations. *Without courage, we are denied the transfusion of innovation that will ultimately determine our future.* Fear also silences many voices at innumerable meetings that take place in countless boardrooms every day. We need courageous, outspoken people.

Frances Hesselbein (Winter, 1997), editor in chief of *Leader to Leader*, president and CEO of the Drucker Foundation, and former chief executive of the Girl Scouts of USA, knows much about the importance of courage in today's business world. In her experience, barriers to leadership are often self-imposed and require courage to lower them. She says:

> "It takes courage for a leader to identify and confront self-imposed barriers, to put in place the personal strategies required to unleash the energy, innovation, and commitment to self-development. It takes equal courage to identify and confront the institutional barriers that limit and inhibit the people of the organization. And it takes real leadership to bulldoze the barriers-frequently time-honored, tradition-bound, deeply ingrained practices."

To be a good leader requires courage, even when ones gut is churning viciously. To be a great leader, one must recognize, acknowledge, and nurture risk takers or would-be risk takers.

After seeing the risks taken by Native American warriors such as Crazy Horse and Colonel Boyington, what most are asked to do pales in comparison. Anyone can be called upon to test his or her courage. How they react is a measure of their ability to lead others.

To earn the Honored Feather of Wisdom for courage:

- Be genuine and take a stand, even on unpopular issues

- Openly express your thoughts to others.

- Recognize and reward the courageous acts of others.

- Take chances even when you know there is a possibility of failure.

- Drive fear from the workplace.

Reflective thoughts

Determination

"Now, Brother, as for me, I assure you I will press on, and the contrary winds may blow strong in my face, yet I will go forward and never turn back, and continue to press forward until I have finished, and I would have you do the same."

—Teedyuscung,
a Delaware

A desire to accomplish something of significance allows us to remove the obstacles that clutter our path. All cultures can point to leaders who were known for their willingness to pursue their dreams with or without the support of others. Native American leaders fought with great determination, against overwhelming odds, to preserve a lifestyle that had served them and their ancestors for millennia.

One of the finest examples of a determined leader was a chief of the Nez Perce. The leader's name was Hinmaton Yalatkit, better known as Chief Joseph. Chief Joseph was a skilled orator, warrior, and leader.

The Nez Perce lived peacefully on their tribal territory in the Pacific Northwest. In 1863, they entered into a treaty by which they agreed to move onto a reservation near Fort Lapwai. In 1877, even though Chief Joseph suggested his people comply with the treaty, many of the people refused. Rather than ignore their decision to resist the treaty, he opted to help them flee to Canada.

Chief Joseph led the Nez Perce on a masterly retreat of over 1,100 miles that ended near Miles City, Montana, only 40 miles from the border of Canada. He fought against overwhelming odds throughout the retreat while caring for the women, children, the aged, the sick and the wounded. His determination in leading his people may have saved them from destruction even though ultimately his fight with the United States was unsuccessful.

The determination of Chief Joseph and his people was evidenced in his famous speech of October 5th, 1877 after their defeat:

> "I am tired of fighting. Our chiefs are killed. Looking Glass is dead. Toohul-hulsote is dead. The old men are all dead. It is the young men who say yes or no. He who led the young men is dead. It is cold and we have no blankets. The little children are freezing to death. My people, some of them, have run away to the hills and have no blankets, no food. No one knows where they are-perhaps freezing to death. I want to have time to look for my children and see how many of them I can find. Maybe I shall find them among the dead. Hear me, my chiefs. I am tired. My heart is sick and sad. *From where the sun now stands I will fight no more forever.*"

It was the Apostle James who wrote, "Faith, if it has no works is dead." No matter what the endeavor, good intentions, without good works, adds up to little or nothing. Today more than ever we need leaders who are willing to take risks even when those risks end in failure. So many societal advances have been made because of what seemed at the time to be failures. Can you imagine the many obstacles that were overcome by people such as the Wright Brothers, Winston

Churchill, Martin Luther King Jr., and other leadership icons? What differentiated them from the masses were their vision and their undaunted determination.

The entire world can relate to the vision of an American icon that had the courage to pursue his dream with great determination. He said, "All our dreams can come true-if we have the courage to pursue them." I was reminded how true his words were when I recently stood with my family next to a statue of this individual holding the hand of a very famous mouse. Of course, I'm talking about Walt Disney.

Walt Disney changed all of our lives for the better. I can vividly recall when, as a young boy, I waited anxiously on Sunday evenings for the Wonderful World of Disney to begin. This was long before we had 24 hour a day cartoon channels. Mickey Mouse, Donald Duck, Goofy, Pluto, Minnie and the other characters were brought to life due to the vision and determination of Walt Disney.

Like so many other successful people, Walt Disney appeared to be a born entrepreneur who never allowed failure to stop him. He earned money at an early age as a paperboy. By the age of 15 he was earning his own way in the world. At the age of 18 he started an art business with only $250.

Walt took a full time job with Kansas City Film Ad in order to earn a steady paycheck until he was ready to start a new business venture. He was a good salesman and he knew the value of networking. He visited many of the people he had met while working in Kansas City in order to get them to invest in him. He raised $15,000 and became president of the Laugh-O-Gram Corporation. In less than a year the corporation went out of business. Walt was left with just his movie camera and a print of his latest movie, *Alice in Cartoonland*. This innovative film combined animated cartoon figures with pictures of a live girl.

He had to give up his apartment and slept in an armchair at the Laugh-O-Gram office. He ate just one meal a day and walked downtown to the Union Station where he paid a dime for a tub bath in a public bathroom. He traded artwork for haircuts and lived for a time on the beans and bread a neighbor gave him.

This was when, according to the Disney legend, he befriended a mouse he named Mortimer who lived off of the crumbs that Walt provided. In July of 1923, at the age of 21, he arrived in Los Angeles in a badly worn jacket and mismatched pants. He had only $40 to his name.

In 1927, Walt Disney began work on a series of cartoons that starred his own creation, *Oswald the Lucky Rabbit*, who soon became a very desirable property. Unfortunately, Disney signed a one-year contract with Charles Mintz that gave Mintz the rights to the name of Disney's creation. After a failed and angry contract re-negotiation with Mintz, Disney is said to have created a new American icon while on a train with his wife Lilly. Walt wanted to name the character Mortimer after his little friend. Lilly hated the name and thus the cartoon character known around the world as Mickey Mouse was named.

Like so many determined people, Walt was a perfectionist who worked 14 hours a day. He dreamed of making an animated cartoon with sound. His dream became a reality when the first Mickey Mouse film opened in New York in September of 1928.

In 1928, *Steamboat Willie* opened as a huge success when Walt Disney was only 26 years old. Disney's initial operation was very small by Hollywood standards. He only earned fifty dollars a week. His operation grew and by the 1930's, when millions of Americans were out of work, Walt prospered. In 1935 the League of Nations presented a medal to Walt Disney, calling Mickey Mouse "a symbol of international good will." Walt Disney and his characters had become world famous.

Disney was always ahead of his time. His idea of making a full-length cartoon movie of *Snow White and the Seven Dwarfs* became known as *Disney's Folly*. But with his creative genius and legendary determination, the rest is history. Many of the attributes of wisdom were also part of Disney's message to the world through the art of filmmaking and animation.

As Disney prospered, he made his studio a great place to work. He provided the best equipment and supplies for his people. He insisted his people call him by his first name. He wanted his company to be a place of warmth and friendliness. He was a family man who built Disneyland because he wanted a fun and clean amusement park where parents could take their children.

During his life, he received more than 30 Motion Picture Academy Awards, and almost 700 other honors. It is said he prized the first Oscar he received above all the other honors. The Motion Picture Academy presented it to him for his creation of Mickey Mouse. When Walt Disney died on December 15, 1966, he was 65 years young and possibly the best-known and best-loved person in the United States.

Determined souls make their vision reality. These are the people who most nobly wear the robes of leadership. Orisen Swett Marden beautifully expresses the importance of the attribute of determination by saying:

> "This force, which is the best thing in you, your highest self, will never respond to any ordinary half-hearted call, or any milk-and-water endeavor. It can only be reached by your supremest call, your supremest effort. It will

respond only to the call that is backed up by the whole of you, not part of you; you must be all there in what you are trying to do. You must bring every particle of your energy, answerable resolution, your best efforts, your persistent industry to your task or the best will not come out of you. You must back up your ambition by your whole nature, by unbounded enthusiasm and a determination to win which knows no failure…only a masterly call, a masterly will, a supreme effort, intense and persistent application, can unlock the door to your inner treasure and release your highest powers."

The elk was symbolic of determination by the Shawnee. The gift of the elk is in knowing exactly what it can achieve by using all of its strength. The elk has great strength, power and stamina. It has the ability to outrun its predators. Elk live in herds and show us how to live cooperatively. People who have the power of the elk are those who use all of their strength in a determined effort to pursue their personal vision.

Just as Native Americans used animals and nature to symbolize the attributes of wisdom, we now have different symbols that remind us of this path. I keep several Disney characters on my desk and a coffee mug filled with pens and pencils that has a picture of Mickey Mouse painting a portrait of Walt Disney (Mickey's Self Portrait). For me, these items symbolize the power of vision and the importance of determination in making dreams come true.

It is through personal determination that we turn our visions into reality.

To earn the Honored Feather of Wisdom for determination:

- Determine your personal vision by asking yourself what you hope to accomplish in the near and distant future.

- Devise a personal plan to make your dreams a reality.

- Have faith that you are capable of accomplishing remarkable things.

- Remember that you are unique and have the seed of greatness within you.

- Be like the elk, make a decision to use all of your strength to pursue your dreams.

- Always remember that the most successful people in the world have been the ones who never gave up.

Reflective thoughts

Experience

"Something is wrong with the white man's council. When the Micmac people used to have council, the old men would speak and tell the young men what to do-and the young men would listen and do what old men told them to. The white men have changed that, too: Now the young men speak, and the old men listen. I believe the Micmac Council was far better."

—Peter Paul, 1865

Native cultures understood the concept of participation versus control. *To gain experience, a wise person understood that mistakes would be made.* A primary difference noted in modern American, as compared to Native American society, was the latter's emphasis on eldership and experience.

Native American and other indigenous cultures listened to their elders. There was value in the words of those who had experienced life. A certain reverence was paid to those who had acquired a great deal of experience.

Our society has pushed away the elderly and forgotten a great deal of experience acquired over the years. We have done a poor job of tapping into their vast pool of knowledge. Rather than spend time with those who have already learned the lessons we seek to learn, we have turned away from them.

Is it a fear of aging or death that repels us from seeking their words of experience? Maybe it is our own sense of self-reliance that keeps us from asking for the advice of others. Could it be that we are so rushed that we neglect the council of others? After all, it does take time to listen.

There is a great deal of experience just waiting to be tapped if we would only take time to listen to what our elders have to say. It was easier to hear the words of our elders when our cultures were less mobile and we lived near family. Today, our families are dispersed to distant locations making meaningful communication difficult. In the absence of the close family unit, we can still reach out to others who can and will share their experiences with us.

A good way to do this is to belong to organizations that assist networking with those who have similar interests. There are many organizations today that are made up of men and women who have gained a great deal of knowledge and who can be helpful. Anyone willing to take the time to establish a meaningful relationship can tap into his or her wise council.

A great deal can be learned from retirees. They are willing to listen and advise if only we ask their help. Many are honored to be asked for their advice. It is as though their experience is so seldom sought that they relish the idea that someone would be interested in what they have to say.

Many businesses today, particularly new start-ups, have learned the value of tapping into the experience of retired business leaders. Organizations such as the *Service Corps of Retired Executives* (SCORE) are available to help entrepreneurs who are willing to listen to the words of retired executives who have traveled similar paths during many years in business. The realization that retired business executives can be of great value may be the reason there are now nearly 400 SCORE chapters located in the United States and its territories.

A great deal of business literature today emphasizes the value of mentorship. There is great value in establishing mentorships, but what about elderships? Many retired or semi-retired men and women would be willing to take on the challenge of assisting someone who really wants to learn.

The value of experience came up recently in a conversation with a close friend who was venting about the poor customer service he had recently received at a department store. He had a question about a product and was treated poorly by a service representative who didn't have the manners to remove a sucker from her mouth while talking to him. When she couldn't answer his question she shouted to another service representative, "Hey Joe, can you help this guy, he has a question I can't answer." Joe couldn't answer the question either so he yelled over to the shift manager who helped my friend.

If you knew my friend, you'd know that he has no problem expressing his concern on nearly any issue. Poor customer service is an issue that gets his attention immediately. He's the type of person who expresses his concern over poor service rather than accepting it as a fact-of-life. He told the store manager he was appalled by the lack of respect and poor customer service he had received. The manager apologized and shared that it was very difficult to find good help these days.

My friend didn't find the manager's answer acceptable. Rather, he sympathized with the manager's predicament and offered her a solution that makes a lot of sense. "Why don't you hire retirees? You could pay them a little more than you are paying new hires and they wouldn't tick off your customers." He explained that there are lots of retirees who understand what it means to provide exceptional customer service. "They have years of experience, and if you also use them as role models for these young men and women you are currently employing, everyone will gain from the experience. Your customers will receive better service, and you'll have better employees."

What he was talking about is a modern form of eldership. This approach allows those who have learned over the years to share their invaluable experience with those who are just learning. What a wonderful way to bring generations together in order to raise the bar on cultural development.

Elders can share their experiences with us while children can show us how to experience new things. To see life through the eyes of a child can be a wonderful experience. As with elders, we can also learn from children.

Children have unique viewpoints that are often ignored by adults. In their eyes, the world is new and exciting. In their eyes, everything is possible, so they aren't afraid of discovering what is impossible. For example, they don't fear computers; they think they are fun to play with. The stroke of a key may lead to some exciting discovery. For many adults, the stroke of a key is something to be feared that may lead to a horrible disaster.

Experience is not limited by age; there are many things we can learn from others regardless of their age. Too often we ignore the experience of others at our own risk.

In Native American cultures, children were not always raised the same way, but there were many similarities in the way they were raised. Ceremonies were used from birth through adulthood to announce the stages and passages of life. According to Leigh Wood (1994):

> "All children were allowed time to play, but they also had to learn, work and train their bodies. Misbehaving children were ridiculed, punished, or frightened into obedience. Each tribe had its own way of living and passed its beliefs and values on to its children. Among the Native Americans today, whether in cities or on reservation, many of these traditional ways continue."

We can learn many valuable lessons from children. Dr. Alan Gregerman (2000), believes there are many gifts and talents that we all possessed naturally as children that are essential to our success as adults. Many of these gifts blend nicely with the attributes of wisdom.

Children can teach us wisdom if we are willing to pay close attention to the special gifts they have to offer. We can learn how to be appreciative or cheerful from children. They can show us how to be courageous and determined. Children seem to understand the importance of listening and they can be totally honest in the way they express themselves. Children show great compassion to others and aren't afraid to share and express their emotions. They have arguments one moment and become the best of friends the next. Children also seem to willingly follow the lead of others when it is appropriate, and they naturally fall into a leadership role when circumstances require it.

We need to tap into the experiences of others. Age and culture shouldn't be barriers to experience, but rather, enhancements that allow us to gain the experience we need in order to grow in wisdom.

Emmett C. Murphy and Michael Snell (1993) cite Sitting Bull as a leader who appreciated the attribute of experience. According to these authors, Sitting Bull knew that a leader had to experience the same things his people did in order to understand their needs and capabilities. It also allowed him to communicate openly with his followers.

He understood that the flow of communication from the bottom-up must be improved and did this by initiating contact with his followers. Sitting Bull was always concerned that communications might somehow get distorted. Such distortion of communications could prove hazardous or even deadly, particularly when dealing with the issue of survival.

By initiating contact with followers, leaders establish listening posts that allow them to check for concerns and situational changes. Here is how Sitting Bull excelled at understanding his followers:

> "To gain this understanding, he "lived the experience of his people," heeding the ages-old admonition that to know a person you must walk a hundred miles in that person's moccasins. Only in this way could he gain full insight into their character and help them confront the challenges and opportunities ahead. Sitting Bull connected at the deepest level with his people, performing the same tasks and living as they lived, claiming no special privilege or exemption from the responsibilities of day-to-day life. He ate what they ate, slept where they slept, and traveled by the same means that they traveled. As a result, he knew firsthand exactly what they could endure and how they would respond in crisis."

Murphy and Snell espoused that immersion in the frontlines teaches an appreciation of differences and an opportunity to study the personalities and behaviors of key players. This empowers the leader with the knowledge necessary to identify unifying themes for mobilizing allies and defeating adversaries. Such experience can make all the difference in any pursuit of excellence.

To earn the Honored Feather of Wisdom for experience:

- To learn something, find others who have already experienced what you want to know. Their insights might prove invaluable.

- Remember that everyone has value. They will share what they know with you if you are only willing to ask and listen.

- Spend time with retirees, they have a wealth of knowledge and they'll willingly share their time with you.

- Spend time with children. Remember that children possess many gifts and talents that can lead us to greater wisdom.

- Join organizations that deal with issues of interest to you. You will meet new and exciting people who will help you grow on many levels.

- Read, read, read, then read some more. There is a wealth of information in books, magazines, journals, and on the Internet. Take time to grow by reading and researching. You'll be amazed by how much you can learn just by taking a little time to stay informed on important issues.

Reflective thoughts

Justice

"Before there were any cities on this continent, before there were bridges to span the Mississippi, before the great network of railroads was even dreamed of, we Indian people had councils which gave their decisions in accordance with the highest ideal of human justice."

—Ohiyesa

According to the Department of Justice, by the end of 1999, the United States had 6.3 million people either on probation, in jail, prison, or on parole. A whopping 3.1 percent of all U.S. adult residents (2,000,000) were locked up in federal, state or local facilities. From 1990 through 1999, the incarceration rate rose faster than the population.

There is a great difference between modern American society and the Native American society of old. In the Native American society of old, a moral law pervaded the tribe. This was a community in which there was no need for locks or doors. Everything was open and easily accessible to the members of the tribe and their visitors.

The act of murder was rare among Native Americans. When it did occur it was considered to be a very grave offense. Atonement was based upon the decree of a council. Judges took all the known circumstances into consideration and if the suspect was found guilty, the murdered person's next of kin was authorized to take the life of the murderer. Quite often, the next of kin would refuse the take the murderer's life and a sentence of banishment was imposed.

Lying was considered to be a capital offense. Someone capable of lying was also considered capable of committing any crime under the guise of cowardly untruth and double-dealing. As such, the destroyer of mutual confidence was summarily put to death, so the evil might go no further. Thievery was seen as a disgrace that carried a stigma that would last throughout a person's life. The Native American concept of justice also carried over into how war was waged.

Connecting the concepts of justice and warfare seems to be an oxymoron. When thinking of the Native American wars, most persons today think of cruelty and revenge. This, of course, has more to do with the illusion of Hollywood than with an accurate concept of Native American warfare. No doubt there were many cases of cruelty and revenge, but warfare as it was practiced by Native Americans was primarily undertaken to develop manly qualities among youths. This was particularly true prior to their introduction into the art of European based warfare. In fact, Native American warfare was often seen as a game in which there was more honor in the degree of risk taken by a warrior than in the number of enemy slain.

Ohiyesa explained that taking the life of an enemy required that the warrior would blacken his face, loosen his hair, and mourn for thirty days. Further, even though it was acceptable to take spoils of war, this did not extend to appropriation of the enemy's territory. There was no intent in war to overthrow another nation or to enslave their people.

There are many stories of how prisoners were treated justly; often they would stay with the tribe that adopted them. Even while Chief Joseph of the Nez Perce retreated eleven hundred miles while protecting the men, women, children and the elderly members of his tribe, he allowed white visitors and travelers to pass unharmed. In one instance, he let them have horses to help them on their way. It must have been very difficult for Native Americans to understand the European type of warfare they would eventually struggle against. The confusion of one warrior was expressed as follows:

> "When a white man kills an Indian in a fair fight it is called honorable, but when an Indian kills a white man in a fair fight it is called murder. When a white army battles Indians and wins it is called a great victory, but if they lose it is called a massacre and bigger armies are raised. If the Indian flees before the advance of such armies, when he tries to return he finds that white men are living where he lived. If he tries to fight off such armies, he is killed and the land is taken anyway. When an Indian is killed it is a great loss which leaves a gap in our people and a sorrow in our heart; when a white is killed, three or four others step up to take his place and there is no end to it. The white man seeks to conquer nature, to bend it to his will and to use it wastefully until it is all gone and then he simply moves on, leaving the waste behind him and looking for new places to take."

—Chiksika, 1779

The lesson here is that we perceive justice based upon our own experiences in life. What was unjust to Chiksika may have been perceived as just by those who wanted to subdue and control the land. After all, Deuteronomy 16:20 said, "Justice, justice shall you pursue that you may thrive and occupy the land." Yet the acts of those who settled the North American frontier are seen by many today as being unjust. Whether it was done justly is still being addressed in our courts even today. Judges are still hearing cases relating to the loss of tribal lands dating back to agreements made over the past 200 years.

To be a person of justice, you must have integrity. What is integrity? Webster's dictionary defines integrity as: "an unimpaired or unmarred condition; an uncompromising adherence to a code of moral, artistic, or other values; utter sincerity, honesty, and candor; avoidance of deception; the quality or state of being complete or undivided."

Integrity is a key part of authentic selfhood. The transition from being a manager to becoming a leader has a lot to do with being authentic. This authenticity requires a leader to exhibit a willingness to question the values and goals of their organization. Integrity is a very important aspect of character. Being a person of integrity means you are guided by a set of moral principles that results in living justly.

If you do not have integrity, you will never be fully accepted as a leader. You will never be totally trusted. You will not be seen as an honest person or as someone who can make the really hard decisions that have to be made during the course of one's lifetime.

Native American leaders were selected as chiefs because they had integrity. They proved their capabilities over the years and members of the tribe voluntarily followed them. Such a leader was Red Cloud who was generally considered the greatest Native American of his time. Even though he was a hereditary chief, he arose to the position by merit.

Red Cloud, during that stormy period in American history showed himself to be a brave warrior, a dignified counselor, a staunch advocate of the welfare of his people, and a person who dealt justly with others. He had the bearing of one who had faced death upon the field of battle. He followed the treaties he agreed upon even when he was given every pretext to violate them. He possessed great kindness, a quiet and gentle demeanor, and lamented the fate of his people without bitterness. He had great integrity.

Integrity is missing from many people and hence, the organizations they belong to. Warren Bennis and Burt Nanus (1985), express how leaders must set the example for their entire organizations. In their words:

> "The leader is responsible for the set of ethics or norms that govern the behavior of people in the organization. Leaders set the moral tone by choosing carefully the people with whom they surround themselves, by communicating a sense of purpose for the organization, by reinforcing appropriate behaviors, and by articulating these moral positions to internal and external constituencies."

This is no easy task. Leaders must spend much time in exhibiting and communicating the behavior they expect from their people. We often find a dichotomy between what organizations do and what they should do if they are acting in a just and ethical manner.

Whistleblowing is becoming very common in today's business environment. It has allowed managers and employees to bring attention to issues of concern that are not addressed by business. We now have a National Whistleblower Center that is committed to environmental protection, nuclear safety, civil rights, government accountability and protecting the rights of employee whistleblowers. The Center was established in 1988 and has successfully established many important precedents protecting employee whistleblowers throughout the United States.

It is truly sad we even need a National Whistleblower Center but we do because justice and integrity are lacking in many organizations. When ethical decisions are not made, employees are forced to blow the whistle on their employers.

The history of humanity is replete with examples of leaders who were just and had great integrity. Tecumseh, Sitting Bull, Red Cloud, and other chiefs are fine examples of Native American leaders who had these attributes and, hence, the loyalty of their people.

To earn the Honored Feather of Wisdom for justice:

- Don't take more than you need and respect the rights and property of others.

- Listen to your heart before you act.

- Treat lying as though it were a capital offense.

- Always tell the truth and expect the same of others.

- Set the moral tone in your organization and surround yourself with others who share your values.

- Express yourself openly, even when it is the unpopular thing to do.

Reflective thoughts

Knowledge

"Knowledge was inherent in all things. The world was a library and its books were the stones, leaves, grass, brooks, and the birds and animals that shared, alike with us, the storms and blessings of earth. We learned to do what only the student of nature ever learns, and that was to feel beauty. We never railed at the storms, the furious winds, and the biting frosts and snows. To do so intensified human futility, so whatever came we adjusted ourselves, by more effort and energy if necessary, but without complaint."

—Chief Luther Standing Bear,
Teton Sioux

"If we wonder often, the gift of knowledge will come."

—Arapaho proverb

Mengelkoch and Nerburn (1991) share the Native American technique that ensured knowledge was passed along from generation to generation. This technique would serve us well today with our families, friends, and co-workers.

> "Traditionally, Indians did not carry on dialogues when discussing important matters. Rather, each person listened attentively until his or her turn came to speak, and then he or she rose and spoke without interruption about the heart of the matter under consideration. This tradition produced a measured eloquence of speech and thought that is almost unmatched for its clarity and simplicity."

Since knowledge and experience went hand-in-hand, the tribal elders stressed the importance of listening and waiting. Training began with children who were taught to sit still and enjoy it. They were taught to use their senses while being quiet. A child who could not sit still was considered to be a half-developed child.

Distinctions were made between learning and becoming knowledgeable. Knowledge was obtained only when one was ready. What one needs to know changes, as they grow older. Growing up is part of the learning experience and with this learning experience came responsibility. Children as well as adults made their own decisions. These decisions were made with a deep understanding of community and nature. Recognizing what we don't understand is the first step towards gaining knowledge.

People can no longer be treated as though we are still in the Industrial Age. People are now required to become thinkers and problem solvers. Their creative ability is a major factor in their usefulness to their company and the economy. *Managers can no longer rely on hierarchical management styles, instead, they must learn to become teachers, coaches, facilitators, and mentors.* This new era of knowledge-based management provides us with unparalleled opportunity for personal and organizational development.

Knowledge based management reminds me of an old-time movie I saw in which a group of students decided to put on a show in order to save their school. Some of them acted and some designed the sets while others made posters and sold tickets. Everyone chipped in to complete the project. Unfortunately, we don't often know the talents of those around us. A Learning Organization strives to know where the talent is and uses that talent to great effect.

In order to put learning power to work, we need to ensure we're training the right people about the right things and in the right way. Many economists agree that training can be a great investment. Numerous studies have been conducted that showed training increased organizational profits. In a Learning Organization it is known where training dollars are going and how the benefits of that training are being used to improve the bottom line.

The Learning Organization is one that fulfills our need to work in a place where we can contribute all the gifts we have to offer. To do that, we need people who are willing to grow and develop their knowledge base. People will willingly evolve if they work for an organization that values knowledge. The Learning Organization is the workplace of the 21st century.

To gain the Honored Feather of Wisdom for knowledge:

- Listen attentively before you speak.

- Remember, the world is a library just waiting for you to immerse yourself in its many lessons.

- When you recognize that you don't understand everything, you've taken the first step towards knowledge.

- Make sure you're learning the right things. Invest your time, energy, and money wisely.

Reflective thoughts

Leadership

"In war, the whites have leaders and war-chiefs of different grades. The common warriors are driven forward like a herd of antelopes to face the foe. It is because of this manner of fighting-from compulsion and not from personal bravery-that we count no coup on them. A lone warrior can do much harm to a large army of them-especially when they are in unfamiliar territory."

—A Santee Sioux

Many persons would argue that leaders are born, not made. You might even think you could never be a leader because you have to be really great, like Martin Luther King, Jr., or John F. Kennedy. These are very traditional viewpoints of leadership, that leadership is an unobtainable, mysterious quality that eludes all but the most gifted members of our society.

Today, however, many theorists believe that leadership is a composite of behaviors that can be learned and used by anyone. There are many aspects of leadership that must be developed to effectively work with others. For example, leadership may require taking responsibility for some action or taking charge of a situation when no one else is able or willing to do so.

In today's dynamic and fast-paced world, we all need to put on the mantle of leadership. We cannot afford to let leadership be a characteristic reserved for only those who hold designated leadership positions. Instead, we each need to know how to lead in our own jobs, regardless of the title that is printed on our business cards.

The first step in becoming a leader is to reflect upon the characteristics you feel a dynamic leader possesses. To do this, think about those people who you perceive as being leaders. Who do you feel are the greatest leaders of all time; were they military, business, or religious leaders? In fact, choose as many leaders as you want. Once you have listed those think of the characteristics that made them great. Chances are, when you cross-reference these qualities, you will find that the really exceptional leaders exemplify many of characteristics you value most.

In Native American leadership, tribal decisions were made by consensus, in which every tribal member participated. Also, chiefs were not coercive, authoritarian rulers, as we tend to think of many leaders today. They were teachers and facilitators, and their duties were confined to specific realms such as medicine, planting, war, relationships, or ceremonies).

Jerry Mander (1991) cites the seminal work of French anthropologist Pierre Clastres from his book *Society Against the State* where Clastres explains his findings on Native American cultures:

> "The chief has no authority at his disposal, no power of coercion, no means of giving an order. The chief is not a commander; the people of the tribe are under no obligation to obey. The chief has to rely on nothing more than the prestige accorded him by the society to restore order and harmony. What qualifies a man to be chief is his technical competence, his oratorical talent, his expertise as a hunter, his ability to coordinate…and in no circumstance does the tribe allow the technical superiority to change into a political authority. The oldest chronicles leave no room for doubt on this score: if there is some-

thing completely alien to an Indian, it is the idea of giving an order or having to obey, except under very special circumstances such as prevail during a martial expedition."

In describing the duties of a chief, Clastres said, "The chief must be responsible for maintaining peace and harmony in the group. He must appease quarrels and settle disputes-not by employing a force he does not possess, but by relying solely on the strength of his prestige, his fairness and his verbal ability. More than a judge who passes sentence, he is an arbiter, who seeks to reconcile."

In 1987, J.M. Kouzes and B.Z. Posner wrote The Leadership Challenge: How to Get Extraordinary Things Done in Organizations." They cited a study of managers in the United States that listed the characteristics they admired most in leaders at work. They came up with the following characteristics:

"Ambitious, broad-minded, caring, competent, cooperative, courageous, dependable, determined, fair-minded, forward-looking, honest, imaginative, independent, inspiring, intelligent, loyal, mature, self-controlled, straightforward, and supportive."

This is a very ambitious list, yet we look for these characteristics in our leaders. To become leaders, we must aspire to emulate the qualities on this list. One way you might do this is to jot down these characteristics and rate yourself on a scale of 1–5, with one being an ordinal rating of "not very" and five being a rating of "very much." How did you rate yourself? Regardless of how you rate yourself, this can be used as a tool for personal development and growth as a leader. If you are managing people now and are feeling really gutsy, let them rate you. We all have room for improvement!

Leadership is quite often a scarce resource in many organizations. It is hard to understand why, particularly with all the talented people who spend such considerable amounts of time at work. It's not as though we've placed some limit on the amount of leadership we are willing to accept: "I'm sorry, we have all the leaders we can handle right now, please exhibit these leadership characteristics on your own time and leave the rest of us alone."

We can all make a difference and become leaders. The real question is: are we willing to step forward and show others that we have what it takes to make a real difference, or are we satisfied with mediocrity?

It is difficult to earn the rights of leadership when your authority rests with the community you are required to serve. Very few people earn that right. The attributes needed to serve a community are extensive. The need to be genuine is paramount if you hope to earn the respect and the voluntary allegiance of others.

The Iroquois Confederacy was made up of several nations. The Confederate Lords might elect any man if he showed great ability and interest in the affairs of the nation. Any man was eligible who proved himself to be wise, honest, and worthy of confidence. But if he ever did anything contrary to council rules, he would not be deposed from office but everyone would be deaf to his voice and advice.

In polling others regarding whom they consider to be the greatest leaders in history, many names are well known. The exploits of these leaders are well documented and usually they have backgrounds based on military, political or humanitarian service. It is unusual to find a leader who has experience in all three of these areas.

Military leaders tend to be great at strategizing and leading their followers into battle. Statesmen are very astute at getting others to play a part in the creation of some great vision that benefits society as a whole. Those who became famous leaders for their humanitarian efforts did so because of their almost limitless capacity to help those in need and their altruistic ideals. In all cases, truly great leaders tended to have an in depth understanding of societal needs and a passionate commitment to make a difference.

One leader, known for his abilities as a great warrior, statesman, and humanitarian, deserves special recognition. He remains a Canadian national hero even though he was born near present day Springfield, Ohio. In fact, many consider Tecumseh to be the greatest Native American leader who ever lived.

Sugden (1997) characterized Tecumseh as a leader who was a successful provider and war chief. Tecumseh also displayed something rare-the judgment, articulateness, integrity, and commitment to the community so admired in a successful chief and counselor.

Sugden explains:

> "A virtue much revered by Shawnees was generosity. Hospitality and the willingness to share food and other resources with the less fortunate were part of every Indian community's ability to survive. Tecumseh was uninterested in personal wealth, and freely gave what he had to those for whom he felt compassion and a sense of responsibility. He was free-hearted and generous to excess, always ready to relieve the wants of others. When he returned from a hunting expedition he would harangue his companions and make use of all his eloquence to instill into their minds honorable and humane sentiments. This, then, was a man able to provide leadership, succor, and understanding, a man

at once inspiring to younger warriors and safe and reassuring to the more vulnerable members of the community."

Sugden admitted that Tecumseh, like all of us, had some faults. Tecumseh could be arrogant, impulsive, haughty, and capable of ruthlessness. But even his enemies remembered his virtues. Even his political opponents praised his character.

Tecumseh's charisma allowed him to attract followers. He was seen as friendly, inviting, and very handsome. He was considered to be a jovial companion and of good humor as were so many other Native Americans. He had a rare and mysterious quality that endeared him to those he came in contact with. As the Governor of the Indiana Territory, who would one day become the chief's greatest adversary, would testify:

"The implicit obedience and respect which the followers of Tecumseh pay to him is really astonishing."

Peter Nabokov (1991) explains that after the colonies were free from England's domination, a remarkable Shawnee leader began rallying many of the same Indians who had previously fought beside the great Chief Pontiac. According to Nabokov:

"His name was *Cougar Crouching for His Prey*, or Tecumseh, and he had earned his warrior's reputation fighting in the defeats of General Harmer at Fort Wayne (1790) and General St. Clair on the Wabash River (1791)."

In the December 2nd, 1820 issue of the *Indiana Centinel* of Vincennes, Indiana, a letter was published that praised the late and hated enemy Tecumseh. "Every schoolboy in the Union now knows that Tecumseh was a great man," it read. "He was truly great-and his greatness was his own, unassisted by science or the aids of education. As a statesman, a warrior and a patriot, take him all in all, we shall not look upon his like again."

Alvin M. Josephy Jr. (1961) stated that by 1846 an American historian, Henry Trumbull, stamped him as "the most extraordinary Indian that has appeared in history," He further points out that the noted biographer, Glenn Tucker, asserted that Tecumseh still looms as the greatest native leader in the long and tragic resistance of the Indians of the United States.

"He was a brilliant orator and warrior and a brave and distinguished patriot of his people. He was learned and wise, and was noted, even among his white enemies, for his integrity and humanity. But his unique greatness lay in the fact that, unlike all previous native leaders he looked beyond the mere resistance by a tribe or group of tribes to white encroachments."

Josephy (1961) explained that Tecumseh understood the value of knowledge. He absorbed the history of Alexander the Great and other leaders of white civilization, pondered over new philosophy from the Bible, and thirsted for even more knowledge that would make him better equipped to understand and deal with the Americans.

Concerning his abilities as an orator, General Sam Dale said:

"His eyes burned with supernatural lustre, and his whole frame trembled with emotion. His voice resounded over the multitude-now sinking in low and musical whispers, now rising to the highest key, hurling out his words like a succession of thunderbolts...I have heard many great orators, but I never saw one with the vocal powers of Tecumseh."

His humanity was shown on several occasions. Josephy (1961) said that many of the Americans had expected to be massacred by the Native Americans after having been captured, but Tecumseh's absolute control over them and his friendly and dignified conduct gradually won the admiration of the prisoners. Later, when they were paroled back to the settlements, they spoke of him as a gallant and honorable enemy. They spread a new concept of him as a humane Indian who had treated captives with consideration.

To better understand why Tecumseh was such a great leader, read the words he left as a message for people. He wrote:

"So live your life that the fear of death can never enter your heart. Trouble no one about their religion; respect others in their view, and demand that they respect yours. Love your life, perfect your life, beautify all things in your life. Seek to make your life long and its purpose in the service of your people.

Prepare a noble death song for the day when you go over the great divide. Always give a word or a sign of salute when meeting or passing a friend, even a stranger, when in a lonely place. Show respect to all people and bow to none. When you arise in the morning, give thanks for the food and for the joy of living. If you see no reason for giving thanks, the fault lies only in yourself. Abuse no one and nothing, for abuse turns the wise ones to fools and robs the spirit of its vision."

Tecumseh was a great warrior who fought for what he believed in and he excelled in the art of warfare. He was a dynamic statesman who traveled as far south as the Gulf of Mexico and as far north as Canada in order to share his dream of a united Native American nation. A true humanitarian, he treated his followers and his prisoners with respect. On several occasions he saved the lives of prisoners who would have been killed without his intervention. Even his staunchest enemies respected him.

Tecumseh is one of the few leaders who truly exhibited the many characteristics that make a leader great. Certainly he earned his place in history as a model of leadership. We can all learn from his example.

Every organization regardless of its size or mission needs leaders such as Tecumseh. We are at a time in history in which we need leaders more than ever. We need them in our for-profit, not-for-profit, civil service, academic, household, and our military settings. In fact, we all need to become leaders, whether we're pushing a broom or designing computer software. It is no longer acceptable to be a non-participant in our organizations.

To earn the Honored Feather of Wisdom for leadership:

- Reflect upon the characteristics you admire most in other leaders and make them your own.

- Be the type of leader who teaches and facilitates others.

- Learn to lead without using coercion or authority. Lead in such a way that people want to follow you.

- Make yourself responsible for maintaining peace and harmony within your organization.

- Rate yourself on Kouzes and Posner's "The Leadership Challenge", and then come up with a personal plan to improve your leadership abilities.

- Remember, there is always room for dynamic leaders in every organization.

Reflective thoughts

Vision

"It is true that I am a Shawnee, my forefathers were warriors. Their son is a warrior. From them I only take my existence; from my tribe I take nothing. I am the maker of my own fortune; and, oh, that I could make that of my red people, and of my country, as great as the conceptions of my mind, when I think of the Spirit that rules the Universe."

—Tecumseh

Tecumseh was a warrior, orator, statesman, and a visionary. During his life he struggled to form a confederacy to win back the lands that had been taken from his and other Native American tribes. It was his vision and the courage to pursue his vision that made him such an exceptional leader. His followers and those who called him enemy respected him. The power of his vision allowed him to come very close to creating a Native American nation. He is still honored today as one of the world's greatest visionary leaders.

Tecumseh used his talent as an orator to share his vision with thousands of followers. This was no easy task when we realize that he spoke to a diverse group of people from different parts of North America.

Truly great leaders, such as Tecumseh, have a mastery of communication that allows them to reach out to all their people and link them together. Mastering multilevel communication is no easy task when we have barriers such as geography, language, and culture to overcome.

Murphy and Snell (1993) believe multilevel communications should emerge naturally from the growth process of building and mobilizing a team and should reflect the experience a leader shares with his or her people.

Some of the finest examples of multilevel communication cited by Murphy and Snell are: Lincoln's *Gettysburg Address*, delivered over fresh graves on the Gettysburg battlefield and "dedicated to the proposition that all men are created equal"; Roosevelt's call to arms after December 7, 1941—"a day that shall live in infamy"; and Churchill's warning to Hitler that "...we shall fight you on the beaches..." delivered over radio just six hours after the British discovered Germany's plan to invade Britain.

This is where the vision begins. It is a platform from which further communication should inspire others to achieve the goals of the leaders vision. As John P. Kotter, author of *Leading Change* stated:

> "In each case, the leader's communication grew out of an experienced need and tightened the nuts and bolts of the social and organizational structure at all levels, strengthening the platform from which the leader could then launch plans of action.
>
> But the real power of a vision is unleashed only when most of those involved in an enterprise or activity have a common understanding of its goals and direction. That shared sense of a desirable future can help motivate and coordinate the kinds of actions that create transformations."

Many leaders have been catalyst of a great vision that has transformed the world. Bob Thomas (1994), author of Walt Disney: An American Original shares with us Walt Disney's vision for Disneyland:

> "The idea of Disneyland is a simple one. It will be a place for people to find happiness and knowledge. It will be a place for parents and children to share pleasant times in one another's company: a place for teachers and pupils to discover greater ways of understanding and education. Here the older generation can recapture the nostalgia of days gone by, and the younger generation can savor the challenge of the future. Here will be the wonders of Nature and Man for all to see and understand. Disneyland will be based upon and dedicated to the ideals, the dreams and hard facts that have created America. And it will be uniquely equipped to dramatize these dreams and facts and send them forth as a source of courage and inspiration to all the world. Disneyland will be something of a fair, an exhibition, a playground, a community center, a museum of living facts, and a showplace of beauty and magic. It will be filled with the accomplishments, the joys and hopes of the world we live in. And it will remind us how to make those wonders part of our own lives."

When Walt Disney passed from this world, no one questioned whether the world was a better place for him having been a part of it. The world mourned. He was called "Aesop with a magic brush", and "a poet-magician who brought the world of fable alive." His vision lives on.

To better understand the role of vision in Native American culture, we need to understand the concept of the medicine shield and how it was used. Among the Native Americans, every man possessed a shield. These personal shields were not just meant for protection. They were a representation of the person who carried them. The signs on the shields told who the person was, what they sought to be, and what they loved, feared and dreamed for.

According to Gerald Hausman (1992):

> "The shield of the mounted warrior of the Plains was an image commonly associated with Native American symbology. Plains Indian shields, roughly two feet in diameter, were made of thick buffalo hide, with one or two covers of soft-dressed buffalo, elk, or deerskin. The design on the outside cover was different from the inside cover. In battle, the warrior loosened and threw back the outside shield cover to reveal the secret symbol within. The shield was then carried on the left arm by means of a belt that passed over the shoulder. Carried in this fashion, the shield permitted the free use of the left hand to

hold a bow, and it also allowed the shield to be slung around to the back, in retreat."

The warrior shield of the Plains Indian was, like a samurai's sword, his most sacred possession. From its first encounter with an enemy to the time it was laid under its owner's head in death, the shield was a thing of power. The shield was believed to have originated from a medicine dream. In the dream, often received by an old warrior, the young man was seen being instructed in making and using his shield. The shield had to be made according to the dream and was painted and decorated in keeping with the wishes of the *Shield Spirit*. This spirit might be a bird, an animal, or a deity of the tribe.

The owner rarely made his own shield; instead, he received it from the dreamer, who made it in trade for horses, blankets, or other property. To make the shield, the protective hide was taken from the neck of a buffalo bull. Extra thickness and toughness were created by wetting and shrinking the hide over a fire built over a hole in the ground. When it was not in use, the warrior's shield was often hung on a tripod of wooden poles that faced the sun.

In addition to providing protection, these shields were a representation or mirror of the person who carried them. The signs on the shields were always kept outside where all could see them. They might be hung by the lodge door, the smoke hole, or on a tripod near the lodge, according to each person's own *Medicine Way*. But they were always kept outside, where the people might see and learn from them. Women of the tribe also carried their *Medicine Signs* in ways to be seen, usually as symbolic designs woven with porcupine quills or beads on their dresses or belts.

Native Americans literally carried and displayed their visions wherever they went. Can you imagine each of us carrying around our personal vision of who we are and who we want to be? Instead of hiding our visions, we could display them openly and unabashedly for the world to see. By doing this, we encourage others to help us make our vision a reality.

To earn the Honored Feather of Wisdom for vision:

- Like Tecumseh, share your vision with others.

- Improve your multilevel communications skills by learning to break down barriers such as geography, language, and culture.

- Create your own medicine shield. Take the time to draw out an artistic representation of your vision.

Reflective thoughts

Reflection

Native America wisdom is a great blessing from the past that provides an opportunity for personal and organizational growth now. Native American wisdom comes to us through their myths and folklore. It was through oratory, rather than the written word that they passed along the attributes of wisdom for our use.

The chiefs of old understood and practiced the attributes of wisdom. It was because they practiced these attributes that they were selected to lead their people. Again, the nineteen attributes of wisdom they practiced were: *appreciation, cheerfulness, compassion, courage, determination, dialogue, experience, honesty, humility, justice, kindness, knowledge, leadership, loyalty, patience, respect, sacrifice, sharing,* and *vision.*

By understanding and practicing these attributes we earn the Honored Feathers of Wisdom. *These feathers symbolize each of the attributes we should continually strive to achieve.* The attributes provide a timeless connection between Native American wisdom, our personal development, and the direction organizations must take in order to provide healthy, happy, and productive work environments.

You cannot earn the Honored Feathers of Wisdom by reading this book. *Wisdom is acquired when we balance what we have learned intellectually with what we know emotionally.* It is this marriage of intellect and emotion that allows us to acquire true wisdom. This balance is needed for us to evolve as human beings. In our own evolution we have the opportunity to bring along the rest of society.

Understanding the attributes of wisdom is not the same as doing them. The world needs more modern-day chiefs. If you understand the attributes of wisdom and are willing to practice them, you will be the type of leader who is needed in the 21st century.

Reflective thoughts

BIBLIOGRAPHY

Ackerman, Diane (1999). *Deep Play*. New York: Random House.

Andrews, Ted (2000). *Animal-Speak: the Spiritual & Magical Powers of Creatures Great & Small*. St. Paul, MN: Llewellyn Publications.

Bear, Sun, Wind, Wabun & Mulligan, Crysalis (1991). *Dancing With the Wheel*. New York: Simon & Schuster.

Beck, Peggy V., Walters, Anna Lee, & Francisco, Nia (1977). *The Sacred: Ways of Knowledge, Sources of Life*. Tsaile, AZ: Navajo Community College Press.

Bennett, William J. (1993). *The Book of Virtues: A Treasury of Great Moral Stories*. New York: Simon & Schuster.

Bennis, Warren & Nanus, Burt (1985). *Leaders: The Strategies for Taking Charge*. New York: Harper and Row.

Brown, Joseph Epes (1997). *Animals of the Soul: Sacred Animals of the Oglala Sioux*. Rockport, MA: Element Books.

Clark, Robert A., & Friswod, Carroll (1976*). The Killing of Chief Crazy Horse*. Lincoln, NE: University of Nebraska Press.

Clastres, Pierre (1977). *Society Against the State*. New York: Urizen Books.

Cleary, Kristen Maree (1996). *Native American Wisdom*. New York: Barnes & Noble Books.

Dahle, Cheryl (2000, January-February) *Mind Games*. FastCompany Magazine, p. 169.

Dickens, Charles (1994). *A Christmas Carol: In Prose Being A Ghost Story of Christmas*. New York: Barnes & Noble Books.

Dyer, Wayne, D. (1998*). Wisdom of the Ages: A Modern Master Brings Eternal Truths into Everyday Life*. New York: HarperCollins Publishers.

Eagle, Rainbow (1998). *The Universal Peace Shield of Truths: Ancient American Indian Peace Shield Teachings*. Angel Fire, NM: Rainbow Light & Company.

Editors of Time Life Books (1975). *The Great Chiefs*. Alexandria, VA: Time-Life Books.

Ellinor, Linda & Gerard, Glenna (1998*). Dialogue: Rediscover the Transforming Power of Conversation*. New York: John Wiley & Sons, Inc.

Greer, Colin & Kohl, Herbert (1995). *A Call to Character*. New York: Harper-Collins Publishers.

Hausman, Gerald (1992). *Turtle Island Alpabet: A Lexicon of Native American Symbols and Culture*. New York: St Martin's Press.

Henderson, Andrew H. LT (1998). *Native American Military Heroes.* Patrick Air Force Base, FL: Defense Equal Opportunity Management Institute.

Hesselbein, Frances (Winter, 1997). *Barriers to Leadership*. New York: The Peter F. Drucker Foundation for Nonprofit Management.

Holton, Bill Ph.D. (1999). *Leadership Lessons of Robert E. Lee: Tips, Tactics, and Strategies for Leaders and Managers*. New York: Gramercy Books.

Isaacs, William (1999). *Dialogue and the Art of Thinking Together: A Pioneering Approach to Communicating in Business and in Life*. New York: Currency.

Josephy, Alvin M. Jr. (1961). *The Patriot Chiefs: A Chronicle of American Indian Leadership*. New York: The Viking Press.

Kaplan, Michael (1998, November). *Sweat et Veritas. GQ*, p. 124.

Kotter, John P. (1996). *Leading Change*. Boston, MA: Harvard Business Press.

Mander, Jerry (1991). *In the Absensce of the Sacred: The Failure of Technology & the Survival of the Indian Nations*. San Francisco: Sierra Club Books.

Maxwell, John C. (1998). *The 21 Irrefutable Laws of Leadership: Follow Them and People Will Follow You.* Nashville, TN: Thomas Nelson Publishers.

Mengelkoch. Louise, & Nerburn, Kent (1991). *Native American Wisdom.* New World Library: San Rafael, California.

Mintzberg, Henry (1975, July-August). *The Managers Job: Folklore and Fact.* Harvard Business Review, pp. 49–61.

Murphy, Emmett C., & Snell, Michael (1993). *The Genius of Sitting Bull: 13 Heroic Stragegies for Today's Business Leaders.* Englewood Cliffs, NJ: Prentice Hall.

Murphy, Emmett C., & Snell, Michael (1994). *Forging the Heroic Organization: A Daring Blueprint for Revitalizing American Business.* Englewood Cliffs, NJ: Prentice Hall.

Nabokov, Peter (1991). *Native American Testimony: A Chronicle of Indian-White Relations from Prophecy to the Present, 1492–1992).* New York: Penguin Group.

Nerburn, Kent (1993). *The Soul of an Indian: And Other Writings From Ohiyesa (Charles Alexander Eastman).* San Rafael, CA: New World Library.

Owusu, Heike (1999). *Symbols of Native America.* New York: Sterling Publishing Company, Inc.

Sams, Jamie (1998). *Dancing the Dream: The Seven Sacred Paths of Human Transformation.* New York: HarperCollins.

Schaef, Anne W. (1995). *Native Wisdom for White Minds.* New York: Ballantine Books.

Schwartz, Tony (November, 2000). *The Greatest Sources of Satisfaction in the Workplace are Internal and Emotional.* FastCompany (p. 398).

Senge, Peter (1990). *The Fifth Discipline: The Art & Practice of the Learning Organization.* New York: Doubleday.

Smithsonian Institute and National Museum of the American Indian (1994). *All Roads are Good: Native Voices on Life and Culture*. Washington and London: Smithsonian Institution Press.

Sugden, John (1997). *Tecumseh: A Life*. New York: Henry Holt and Company.

Tannen, Deborah (1994). *Talking From 9 To 5: How Women's and Men's Conversational Styles Affect Who Gets Heard, Who Gets Credit, And What Gets Done At Work*. New York: William Morrow and Company.

Terr, Lenore, M.D. (1999). *Beyond Love and Work: Why Adults Need to Play*. New York: Scribner.

Tuchman, Gail (1994). *Through the Eye of the Feather: Native American Visions.*: Layton, Utah: Gibbs Smith, Publishing

Van Housen, Alice (1997, August-September). *Here's a Radical Idea—Telling the Truth!* FastCompany Magazine, p. 50.

Wall, Steve & Arden, Harvey (1990). *Wisdomkeepers: Meetings with Native American Spiritual Elders*. Hillsboro, OR: Beyond Words Publishing.

Weinstein, Matt (1996). *Managing to Have Fun*. New York: Simon & Schuster.

Wheatley, Margaret (Summer, 1997). *Goodbye, Command and Control*. New York: The Peter F. Drucker Foundation for Nonprofit Management. Leader to Leader.

Wood, Leigh (1994). *Native American Culture: Child Rearing*. Vero Beach, FL: Rourke Publications.

0-595-29991-1

Printed in the United States
38609LVS00004B/55